Editor's Letter

It's a dog's life...

Hello readers! Arnold here, the editor of *Bitch*, Big Town's best canine read. We've got tons of stuff to offer the discerning dog about town in this month's issue, especially if you like hot bitches. We've got hot bitches of all kinds and sizes, including Fruity the horny little terrier, Flossie the long-legged supermodel, and the finest in upper-class crumpet in the shape of Tara and Prunella. But *Bitch* is not just about the cynical titillation of your basest urges in order to shift magazines. That's why we've got articles on stuff like bones and kennels and rubber toys and licking your arse and all that sort of thing. This means we continue to offer you, the reader, the very best in woof-related journalism and photography, and you can tell everyone you read *Bitch* for the articles about bones and kennels and rubber toys and licking your arse, rather than just to drool over pictures of hot bitches that want to do it with you.

Talking of hot bitches that want to do it with you, don't forget to read our outrageous exposé on the appalling and degrading spectacle that's sweeping our once decent town. It's called dogging and there's no gratuitous sex with strangers involved. None whatsoever. It's truly awful. It really is.

So sit back, chew on your favourite chewy thing, scratch your mite-infested ears with your back leg and indulge yourself in this month's *Bitch*. And if you don't like it, you can shove it where the sun don't shine. I think we understand each other.

Picture assistant Glenda
Tea dogs Prince and Toby
Advertising manager Smiffy
Advertising executive Amber
Classified sales Bubbles

Contributors Lycos, Lara, Norton, Fruity, Piper, Drummer, Luke, Jaffa, Seamus, Leela, Hooch, Bleu, Randall, Cubby, Possum, Jaz, Buddy, Sophie, Macky Valentine, Queenie, Rolo, Saffy (Homebrood Snow White), Bridie (Dreamweaver By Hearthfriend), Peggy-Sue (Hearthfriend Hi Jinks), Sasha, Flourie, Pebbles, Zeta, Emma, Annie, Millie, Lucy, Tazz, Sam, Poppy, Mercedes, Oscar Willis (Titan Of Occold), Arnold Willis (Golden Royal One), Wilson, Alfie, Lucky, Bob, Keddy, Bilbo, Bess, Milo, Roxi, Beanie, Rip, Molly, Sumo Snuffle McWaffle IV and Big Dog
Cats Misty-Woo Willis and Spike
Rabbit Shade Willis
Horse Dolly
Geese Burton and Harris
Chicken Bernard
Sheep Baaarbara and Minty

Contact *Bitch* at:
The Bins Round The Back Of The Butcher's Shop,
Big Town
AK9 GRRR

No part of this publication may be reproduced, stored in a retrieval system or transmitted in any form whatsoever without the written permission of the editor. Unless you slip me some bones on the quiet. Have you got any bones? Or perhaps some meat? I'll take a handful of those processed choccie drops if that's all you've got. I like them cos they've got dog drugs in them and make me go mad in my head. The last time I had them, I ate a whole packet and went on a violent rampage that only ended when a tranquilliser dart was shot into my bum. Now *that* was a night out.

All models are over 18 weeks old

This month's contributors

TAZZ
"Shit is my life," says the author of our Turder Prize piece. "I love it, me. Brown poo, white poo, the lot." That's what we call a professional.

POPPY
A showbiz journalist doesn't just munch free Bonios with the rich and famous at glittering parties, as Poppy proves in this month's issue.

BREATHLESS DAWSON
Breathless comes to *Bitch* from *Fighting Quarterly*, where he wrote about aggro brilliantly. He is nine and deaf in one ear.

Page 46: Spotty

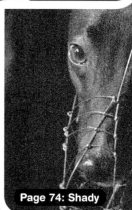

Page 74: Shady

DO IT
YOUR
SELF

Old English Sheepdog
Popular Front

LETTERS

Bones, bollocks and bonking are among the topics our readers are talking about this issue.
To have your say, write to:
Bitch Letters, The Bins Round The Back Of The Butcher's Shop, Big Town, AK9 GRRR

GIVE IT A REST, GRANDPA

To Whom It May Concern,
I can't allow what I saw in the last issue of *Bitch* to pass without comment. It's all very well for you media types to make sweeping generalisations about the rest of canine life, but you ought to stick your noses out beyond your exclusive watering holes and take a look at the real world. I mean, while you lot are sitting in your trendy loft apartments, dining on Cesar (Beef Teriyaki flavour, watered down with the finest sake, no doubt) and going for walkies in exclusive parks with owners who use diamond-encrusted poop scoopers inlaid with gold-leaf details of a hunting scene copied with great care and attention from a painting hanging in the Big Town portrait gallery by the finest craftsmen in the region, the rest of us have to deal with a slightly more down-at-heel reality than your swanky, snazzy, jazzy, jet-setting, celebrity bed-hopping, platinum-pampered, so-called "lifestyle". You make me sick, with your snooty attitudes and your neatly clipped claws, your bright eyes and moist noses, your boundless energy and your rubber chewy toys. You disgust me.
Deputy Dawg, Big Town Sheriff's Office
THE ED SAYS: Sheesh. I think Muskie the Muskrat must have been on Ty Coon's melon patch again.

STAR LETTER

COMPLAINER

BONE CONTROVERSY

Dear *Bitch*,
I had seven bones. I ate one, lost one near the gasworks (well, that was the last place I saw it, anyways), gave two to Fifi La Trix for "special services", and buried the rest somewhere I've now forgotten. How many bones do I have left? And where are they?
Rufus, Big Town Dog's Home And Crematorium
THE ED SAYS: You really are a doofus, Rufus. You have three bones left. At least, you would have done if Elmer hadn't seen you burying them in the field with the daffodils beside the ring road. He dug the bones up and ate two of them straight away. He buried the third in the woods. Or maybe in the park. Or maybe in Mr Pilkington's vegetable patch.

WHAT A LOAD OF BOLLOCKS

Dear *Bitch*,
Have any other readers noticed how great licking your own testicles is? I usually lick mine four or five times every day. More at the weekends.
Harry, 28 Main Street
THE ED SAYS: Good for you. Don't forget your anus while you're down there, will you?

WHAT A BUNCH OF PUSSIES

Wotcha *Bitch*,
The other day, I chased a cat across three gardens and up a tree. I circled around the bottom of the tree barking and growling while the cat stared at me intently, its long tail swiping the air like an angry pendulum. Eventually I got bored and wandered off, but not before I'd cocked my leg up the trunk. The thing is, when I told my right-on mates about my adventure, they were not impressed. They told me chasing cats just isn't on anymore and that it's "like, not cool, dude". What is the world coming to?

Is it some sort of PC hippy nonsense gone crazy? Next you'll be telling me that they are going to ban fox hunting. Or that dog fighting in a sawdust ring in a warehouse on the edge of town surrounded by baying men covered in dodgy tattoos who carry illegal weapons and deal in stolen goods is somehow wrong.

Bruiser, The Big Town Ruffians Club

THE ED SAYS: Bruiser, you're a Pitbull – and it's only because we're frightened of you that we're not going to point out that everything you do is either against the law or extremely anti-social. That said, we all know chasing cats up trees is just a harmless bit of fun that the cat enjoys as much as we do.

SMELLY RED THING
Dear Sir/Madam,

I love my favourite rubber chewy bone. It's brilliant. It's covered in my old drool and it really stinks. It's red.

Fanny, 33 The Villas

THE ED SAYS: Do any other readers have a favourite toy? Perhaps you've got a tatty old slipper with which you've made some kind of unfathomable and obsessive bond. Or maybe your best friend's a frisbee. If so, why not send us a picture of yourself and your stupid toy. You might win a prize. At the very least, you'll give us a laugh.

BOTHERSOME HIPPY
Green Greetings!

I would like to draw your attention to an issue which affects each and every one of us. This, you see, is a global issue. There is not one dog in the whole of Big Town for whom this is not important. I am speaking about the de-forestation of Big Town. It is an appalling situation. As each year passes, we lose another vast swathe of trees. The ones down the precinct were replaced by concrete bollards last April and, even as I write this now, the Big Town Woods are being savagely stripped by the corporate greed of Mr Pilkington's Arts And Crafts Handmade Bespoke Furniture Society For Elderly Gentlefolk. If Mr Pilkington and his chainsaw-wielding goons carry on ripping

out our natural resources at this alarming rate, there will only be 400,000 trees left by the end of the decade. Then where will you cock your leg? I'll tell you where. On some corporate pissing unit made of old CFC-loaded deodorant cans, that's where. And you'll have to pay for it. Our way of life is under threat. Protest and survive!

Dylan, Big Town Hippy Commune

THE ED SAYS: We asked Mr Pilkington if he wanted to respond to your comments, but he said he was too busy shagging Mrs Johnson, the bank manager's wife.

SEX, SEX, SEX, SEX, SEX
Hello *Bitch*,

I've enclosed a photo of me scratching at the French doors. I spend a lot of my time doing this. My owner, Mrs Johnson, locks me outside for an hour every Wednesday afternoon, when Mr Pilkington comes to our house for tea and crumpets. She also locks me out on Friday mornings (when the milkman collects his money), Thursday nights (when Dr Carson comes to check her chest) and all day Mondays (when the Big Town football team pop over). I am, however, allowed to stay inside the house whenever Mr Johnson is at home – apart from two five-minute periods every year, once at Christmas and once when it's Mr Johnson's birthday.

Wendy, 16 Acacia Avenue

THE ED SAYS: Get a haircut, wacko.

Wendy: "Lemme in!"

Sheep, yesterday

WOOLLY IDIOTS
Dear *Bitch*,

I wonder how many readers are, like me, enthusiastic sheep worriers? This ancient traditional activity seems to be in decline, which is a great shame because very few other dog pastimes are so satisfying. Only the other day, for example, me and Bonzo went out to the Big Town sheep field and told the stupid woollies about how their civil liberties are being gradually eroded by a government that is intent on introducing new legislation allowing them to be jailed without proper sheep trials and without even knowing why they've been interned. That put the willies right up them, I can tell you. If anybody fancies joining in with the fun, just come along to Bonzo's kennel on Saturday, when we'll be popping down the sheep field to tell them about wolves, nuclear proliferation and global warming. We also generally meet up on the second Monday of the month, which we call Mint Sauce Monday.

Harvey, 91 Long Lane

THE ED SAYS: Nice one, Harvey. And may we remind readers that if sheep worrying is not thrilling enough for you, you can always join Bruiser's brand new club. It meets every week behind the Big Town Cock Fighting Facility. For further information, contact Bruiser c/o The All-Night Livestock Slaughtering Club (Sheep Division), Behind The Big Town Cock Fighting Facility, Big Town.

FETCH!

EVERYTHING YOU NEED FOR A DOG'S LIFE

SPUGGY CATCHES STICK SHOCKER!

There was jubilation yesterday when Spuggy caught this enormous stick in the try-outs for the Big Town Olympic fetching team. It is thought that the stick, found in long grass near the woods, is the largest stick in the world, although this is yet to be verified.

"I've been in training for a year now," Spuggy told the waiting press scrum after he'd tried to run through a doorway still grasping the absurdly long stick in his mouth and nearly knocked his own head off. "I was confident I could make it this time," he added. "I've been catching stupidly huge sticks for over a year now and have got pretty good at it."

Spuggy's stick-fetching talents represent the best chance for Big Town to win a medal in the forthcoming Olympics, after the shitting team collapsed in disarray in the wake of Rex's nasty bout of diarrhoea.

The Loyal Family

They wear diamond-studded collars and live in the largest house in Big Town, but what do we really know about the members of the Loyal Family?

WILLIAM
PACK ROLE: SECOND HEIR TO THE BONE

The eldest pup of Prince. Adored by bitches the length and breadth of Big Town. Looks remarkably like his mother, the irreplaceable Lady (the queen of all our hearts, *Candle In The Wind*, etc), and is a favourite target of the *puppyrazzi*. Went to Big Town University to study digging up old bones and was happy to muck in with all the other students, regardless of their pedigree.

HARRY
PACK ROLE: UNRULY PUP

Prince's second pup, although for reasons not known, he doesn't really bear much resemblance to his father. Got into a lot of trouble for dressing up as an Alsatian at a fancy dress party. Was at the centre of another controversy when discovered off his choppers on Bob Martin's vitamin pills. Was also said to have been "helped" to pass his obedience test by the late and great Barbara Woodhouse (RIP). In the army now, mainly to try to keep him out of the newspapers for a while.

DUKE
PACK ROLE: CURMUDGEON

Consort to Queenie. Famous for making stereotyping comments about other breeds ("Duke Sticks His Paw In It Again" screamed a recent headline in The Guardog). Likes fetta cheese. And olives. And Demis Roussos. And Nana Mouskouri. Patron of Big Town's Worldwide Fund For Nature. Especially fond of pheasants.

QUEENIE
PACK ROLE: LEADER

Big Town's top dog. Well known for her *anus horriblus*, which is certainly not to be sniffed at. Extremely old because she has two birthdays a year, meaning that she gets 14 years older every 12 months. Something like that, anyway. Addresses Big Town every Christmas Day, mainly so she can describe her *anus horriblus* in great detail. Likes pheasants and horses. Keeps her dog biscuits in Tupperware containers. Did we mention the *anus*? Oh, right, sorry. Michael Canine once sat on her bed. *(Are you sure? – Ed)*.

PRINCE
PACK ROLE: HEIR TO THE BONE

The eldest pup of Queenie and Duke. Large and not a little flappy in the ear department. Wanders around Big Town chatting to plants and endlessly banging on about traditional kennel designs. Likes pheasants and anything Welsh, but was overheard muttering that he "can't stand" Nicholas, the red-furred BBC newshound. Said to be twisted with rage at Queenie for not giving up the bone, despite the fact that she's now aged 1092.

CAMILLA
PACK ROLE: GRUDGINGLY ACCEPTED NON-CORGI

Prince's latest squeeze. Replaces the irreplaceable Lady (the queen of all our hearts, *Candle In The Wind*, etc). Prince has reportedly been "special friends" with Camilla for donkey's years – even when she was mating with both Parker (Lady Penelope's dog) and also Bowles (who lives on Main Street). Although a Pug rather than a Corgi, she's still a toff and so she probably owns a butt-load of Big Town real estate.

Dogging

The Sordid Truth
A special report by STAN COLLIE

There's a disgusting new craze sweeping through Big Town. And we here at *Bitch* feel that it's our duty to write about this vile behaviour in hysterical tones of moral outrage.

In order to fully expose this depraved nocturnal world, we need to devote a two-page spread to a special report by our special reporter Stan Collie and a large photograph of this ugly night-time hobby. In future issues of *Bitch*, we'll probably initiate some kind of dogging section, where readers can send us snaps of their own dogging activities and recommend good dogging venues for future meetings. We might also include several pages of lucrative small ads, through which readers can make contact with other dogs who share their perverse interests. By taking these radical measures, we intend to thoroughly investigate the decay in our society that dogging represents and reverse this repulsive trend. In colour, with a bit of luck.

What, then, is dogging? We were hoping to find acres of dogs in a writhing orgy of anonymous sex, all howling and barking in canine ecstasy under a full moon. This abominable phenomenon would, we'd assumed, recall the Old Times, when dogs roamed the world in vast packs and worshipped the ancient god Lassie. Their pagan celebrations would last several days, with many cats being offered up as ritualistic sacrifices while the dogs danced around going, "Woof! Woof!" and "Grrrr!"

So we were horrified to discover that this new passion called dogging turns out just to be a load of dogs meeting up in car parks to run around and sniff each other's arses.

"But it's great fun!" protested Spike, a three-year-old Alsatian who has been an enthusiastic dogger for six months. "We get to wizz up car tyres and everything."

It is, we're sure you'll agree, a sickening situation.

We MUST act now.

We MUST stop this filth.

FETCH!

Every issue, Timmy gets his chops around an arse you all know and love. Can you guess whose bottom this is? Bet you can't get it out of your head. You'd certainly be lucky, lucky, lucky to find your nose buried between these butt cheeks. After all, everybody needs good Neighbours. Even Timmy, who's just been placed on the sex offenders register.

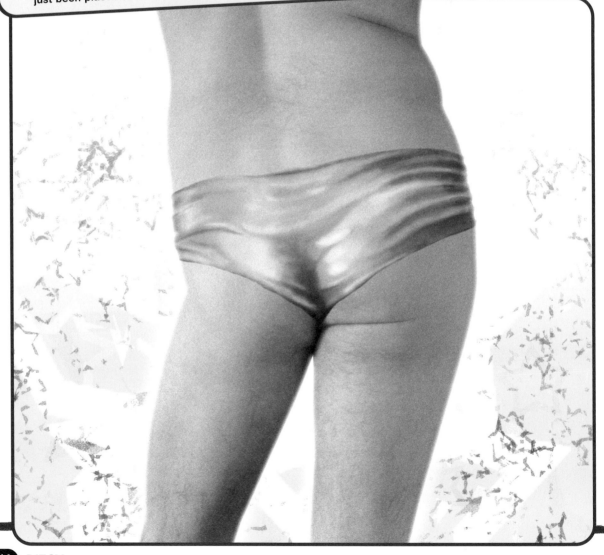

in the beginning...
there was bone

BONELYS
BURYING SERVICES

Your kennel may be at risk if you do not keep up repayments. Either that or we'll send Bruiser round to give you a sound kicking

POND SCUM

_17 59_

PURE DETRITUS

THIS IS: DJ BOUNCE

The jet-set lifestyle, the bitches, the record company A&R consultancy and the arse-crushingly tedious radio show on Big Town FM for which he was vastly over-paid. He thought it would all last forever, but that's what necking too many disco biscuits does for you…

What sort of style are you rocking this week?
It's strict grime, but with a kind of new wave rock vibe, like Franz Ferdinand mixed with Lady Sovereign. I might drop a big party tune every now and then, something by Steps or Napalm Death, say, but I generally like a bit of classic garage. A monster tune at the moment is Status Quo's *In The Army Now*, for example.

Didn't you make your name as a house DJ?
No, house is out of fashion.

I'm sure you were once known as the "Dog Of House"…
Don't you mean the "Dog Of Kennel"?

I thought that was MC Fido…
Well, I've never been into house music or kennel music. Honest. It's always been grime with a new wave edge for me. I'm always ahead of the curve. I mean, I was into Franz Ferdinand and The Libertines before they even formed. Is it still OK to like Franz Ferdinand? Who won the Mercury Prize this year?

Some say that DJing is incredibly easy because all you're doing is playing records. In fact, now that most DJs are using CDs and iPods, I've heard that it helps if you're an absolute twat-faced spooge-head with no discernible talent whatsoever.
No, that's not right. It's very difficult to play records. It might look as though I'm just noncing around, pressing a button every now and then, spending all my time drinking and eyeing up the bitches, but it takes real, erm, skill to put a set together.

How much money did you earn last year?
Three quid.

Wow! You must live a jet-set lifestyle!
Yeah, it's great. I'm great, me.

You are actually.
Yeah, I know. I'm great, me.

On the other hand, your last so-called "artist album", *For God's Sake, Please Buy My Album, I Have Got An Enormous Mortgage Because I Thought That Dance Music Would Last Forever And All I Had To Do To Maintain This Preposterously Lavish Lifestyle Was Slap A Few Mediocre Tunes Together On

A Laptop And Buy Some Clothes In Tokyo crashed out of the charts after selling a mere 12 copies.

What's your point?

My point is that you're a clueless old idiot whose career appears to be over.
That's as might be, but there has always been a new wave rock element to my dance music.

That's not true, is it?
No. Can I go walkies now?

A DAY IN THE LIFE OF
A SNIFFER DOG

"My job mostly involves my nose. I basically spend all of the time sniffing. Which is ace because I seem to have a real talent for it. It just comes naturally to me. Even when I'm not actually working, I still do quite a bit of sniffing. Recreational sniffing, I call it.

"I like to keep my nose nice and wet because it's obviously important that I take good care of it. It's not the only tool of my trade, though. There's also my tail, which I wag like crazy whenever I smell something interesting. Mind you, wagging my tail comes naturally to me, as well. I reckon I was born to do this job.

"I work shifts, which is tons better than having to do the same hours day in, day out. I don't know how those nine-to-five dogs stand it. It would drive me round the flipping bend. I get a huge buzz when I see my master putting on his peaked cap and his shiny black shoes. Actually, now that I think about it, I get lots of huge buzzes when I'm working. I guess that goes to show how much I love my job, doesn't it?

"The place I work is full of big metal birds. They're landing and taking off all day long. I've no idea why, but I thought I'd mention it anyway. There are always loads of humans wandering around, usually carrying heavy bags. My job is to jump on the bags to see if I can smell anything interesting inside. It's great fun. Sometimes I even get to ride on one of the conveyor belt things that goes round and round and round. I especially like it when the conveyor belt's empty but there's still one human standing beside it yelling, 'Where the fuck's my fucking bag, you fucking fuckers?'

"I don't think there's such a thing as an average day for me. It's partly because of the shift work, of course, but there are other factors as well. My moods, for example, which change all the time. Sometimes I get a warm feeling in my tummy, like I've just been tickled. I'll dance around in these little circles, nodding my head and making repetitive movements with my paws. Sometimes I lose my appetite and I can't stop barking and my old todger stays hard for hours and hours and hours. But then at other times, I feel dead sleepy and can't get out of bed in the mornings. I'll giggle at things that aren't even funny and have cravings for toast. I worry that the big metal birds are out to get me and I forget, erm… I forget what I, erm… Oh, I'm sorry, I've lost track of what I was flipping talking about…

"If I smell something interesting in a bag, my master usually takes it away to a warehouse and the human that owns it has to go into a special room where everybody is wearing rubber gloves. My master doesn't take all of the smelly bags to the warehouse, though. He brings some of them home with him and they're collected in the middle of the night by a man who has a white BMW with tinted windows and a long scar down his cheek. The man always gives my master a brown envelope when he leaves.

"What I like best about my job is that I get plenty of holidays. I am on holiday at the moment, as it goes. I haven't worked for a few weeks now. Not since a group of my master's pals came to the house early one morning. I know they were his pals because they all wore peaked caps and shiny black shoes.

"Anyway, they took my master away in a car. I couldn't tell you what sort of car it was but it had a blue light on the roof. Actually, now that I think about it, I haven't seen my master since then…"

EXCLUSIVE INTERVIEW

MY NAME IS

MICHAEL CANINE

I'd like to begin by asking a question about one of your classic early works, *Alfie The Afghan*. Were you surprised to get the part? You are, after all, a Daschund not an Afghan, aren't you?
Not a lot of people know that.

After *Alfie*, you starred in *The Italian Dog*. But you were only chosen for that movie because you were small enough to fit in a Mini, weren't you?
Not a lot of people know that.

Two of your best known films are *Get Rover* and *Educating Fido*, but I think they're both a load of rubbish. In fact, I think you're a load of rubbish and I'd like to challenge you to a fight round the back of the library next Tuesday. And I'm bound to win because I'm a Great Dane. What do you say to that, then, Michael bloody Canine?
You're a big dog, but you're out of shape. For me it's a full-time job.

DOG-MA

Every month, we invite readers to send us photographs of their mothers. This issue, Benji has sent a snap of his mum Sophie.

ALAN vs PREDATOR

Round 17: The winner is Predator. Again.

THE PUPPY GUIDE
Number 7: LEG HUMPING

You will be rewarded with a lifetime of inappropriate sexual gratification if you perfect this skill early in life. First, sniff the trail. Hmm, is that stinky trainer? Why, yes it is! And where there are stinky trainers, there are humpable legs. Just wrap those little paws around the leg and – wahey – off you go! Get some in, my son!

Filth®...

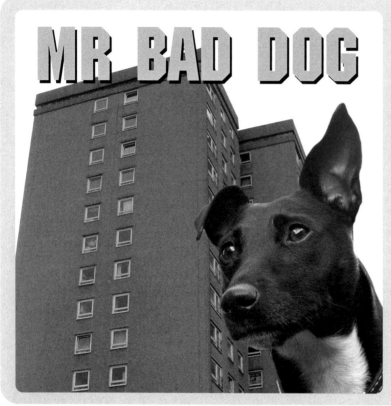

MR BAD DOG

Mr Bad Dog is the most notorious resident of Big Town's inner city housing projects. Usually seen wearing a red neckerchief and strutting about like a robber's dog packing heat, Mr Bad Dog has teeth like razors and the sinister charisma you'd expect from a muscular killing machine.

He is, of course, best known for savaging Gnasher during the Big Town Poetry Riots of last summer, when Gnasher threw down the now legendary rhyme: *"Mr Bad Dog/He is rubbish/As a dog/He is nish"*. Mr Bad Dog responded with a swingeing critique of his opponent's work, accusing Gnasher of using "bankrupt forms, poor quality rhymes and out-dated street language". The public row effectively ended Gnasher's career, turning the former Savage Dog Poet Laureate into a laughing stock. He was last seen getting on the 65 bus to the railway station with his tail between his legs.

Mr Bad Dog went on to deliver *Meat*, a devastating piece which has been adopted as the official poem of Big Town's Association of Fighting Dogs and Violent Strays. It goes: *"Meat!/Give me meat!/Or I'll eat your bloody feet/I will/I'm not joking"*.

TEARING SHIT UP
Number 4: NEWSPAPERS

When tackling your owner's daily read, it is essential to set upon it within seconds of it landing on the doormat. An arched back is advisable and, if possible, mad staring eyes fixed on the paper boy. Note the release of heavy drool. Rip the newspaper's head off by violently shaking it while growling like a prize nutter. Good job!

Stench®…

FETCH!

BRUTUS SPLASHES IT ALL OVER

Brutus in action

Ah, the great joy of cocking a leg and letting go all over somewhere that a human will later want to sit and eat their lunch. Here I am, pissing all over a post in the new bus shelter. Arf! Arf! Oi! Stop pulling!

NOISE ANNOYS

A list of rackets that turn us into doggy howlers

1. A dog whistle… As heard on *One Dog And His Man*. One toot and you'll be hunting for the nearest sheep.
2. A harmonica… Your owner thinks it's funny to puff into it, but it drives you bananas.
3. Christina Aguilera singing on the telly… Yowsa!
4. An old kettle… Milk, no sugar please.
5. The moon… You just can't help howling at it. This one is OK, though, because it's perfectly natural.

ALTERNATIVE LIFESTYLES EXPOSED

Big Town's perverted secrets revealed by *puppyrazzi* photographer Lenses McFadden

Cat!

wabbit!

Another Cat!

A HOMELESS IS FOR LIFE
NOT JUST FOR CHRISTMAS

And with interest rates the way they are, there's soon going to be a lot more of them

My Blanket®

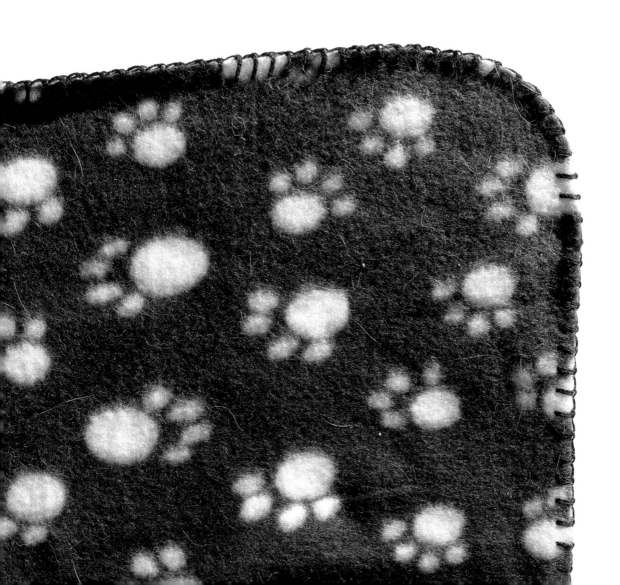

FRIEND OR FOOD?

An indispensable guide to the farmyard by our Countryside correspondent Jethro Inbred

This here creature on the left here, he be a cock. He don't be a big cock, but he still be a cock all the same. He walk aboot the farm all day and he go "cluck cluck" and peck at the floor and he go "cockle doodle doo!" rilly, rilly loud when the old sun come up first thing in the morning. He also shag his hens when he can. Them say he make for roight tasty eating, but his name be Frank and he be my mate, so you don't want to go eatin' him.

Them two white sort of duck sort of things on the left, them two be gooses. They go "honk honk" and hiss and try to bite you while they're running aboot with their necks stretched all the way out and their wings flapping aboot and all. They say what be good for the goose be good for the gander, but them gooses they like farting and I bain't heard of no gander what likes that. Them names be Gloria and Nigel and them be my mates, so don't you go eatin' them.

FRED MAN

FOOD

This here be an horse called Michael Horse. Them be big old critters what go "neigh neigh" and stamp their feet on the floor and run aboot going rilly, rilly, rilly fast. Sometimes they looks at you across the fence and calls you all names. Michael Horse calls me a twat. Many dogs think this be a friendly type of beast and reckon we should be mates with them. On the hole this is the troof. However, I have it on the highest aufority that this animal is sometimes chopped up into littel pieces and shoved into cans what then gets "Dog Food" writted on them. You'll be eatin' Michael Horse tonight probably. Serves the old bugger roight.

BIG DOG

This month, Big Dog goes to the beach. Next issue, in the final instalment of our gripping series, Big Dog goes to the vet's.

suck *pfff* *suck*

OLD DOG: NEW TRICKS?

In a startling new piece of scientific research performed by Dr Dogz, research fellow of Stupid Dogology at the Big Town Institute, it has been proved that, contrary to prevailing paradigms of dogology, it's not possible to teach an old dog new tricks.

"We took Alfie, a 14-year-old boxer whose tricks repertoire amounted to sitting and 'shaking hands', and tried to teach him how to ride a unicycle while juggling with three chainsaws," Dr Dogz told us yesterday. "Unfortunately, he only managed to get six yards before he lost control of one of the chainsaws and it sliced his head off. It was his own fault."

Alfie: Could not learn new tricks and died

POLL OF THE MONTH

What are the most popular paw-twitching doggie dreams?

1) Chasing cats – the old classic

2) Chasing rabbits

3) Eating homework

4) Sniffing another dog's bum

5) Fetching slippers

6) Chasing cats again

7) Finding dinosaur bone

THE DOG'S BOLLOCKS

Thanks to Walter (the white one) who has sent a picture of himself with his pal Tosh for our monthly humiliation of a reader who is rubbish at some aspect of being a dog. "Tosh is bollocks at barking," says Walter. "I hate him."

WHIMPERING: A MEMOIR

It was the summer of 1939, shortly before the war. Whimpering was all the rage in those balmy weeks before Hitler and his evil hordes changed our lives forever. I remember having lots of splendid whimpering parties on the camomile lawns of Charlie's aunt's. I do recall, however, Nancy humiliating herself by howling. Oh, it was all such fun.

BIG TOWN BEACH
A Scavenger's Paradise

- ✿ DIG YOUR OWN VERY BIG HOLE
- ✿ ENDLESS SPACE TO RUN UNTIL YOU DROP
- ✿ FREE PICNIC TAKEAWAYS (AT YOUR OWN RISK)
- ✿ LOTS OF OLD ICE CREAM CONES WITH ALL ANTS AND THAT
- ✿ SAVAGE CHILDREN WITH IMPUNITY
- ✿ RABIES-FREE SINCE 2003

ARNUS
TOURS
YOU HAVEN'T SHIT UNTIL
YOU'VE SHIT ON SAND

Wish you were here!

WHERE DID YOU P[

Our latest contestant is Scooter, the 2002 champion, who is trying to find his bone in a Category 2 sized garden

left a bit, left a bit...

do you need glasses?

what are you doing, you plonker?

locked on target... keep a straight line

it's no use just shaking your head

about bloody time

‑ THAT BONE?

Matchplay Analysis by Lawrence

"I know it's a cliché, Gary, but this really was a game of two halves. Scooter began very badly – so badly that it's hard to believe he's an experienced bone hunter. Let's not forget that he won the title back in 2002. As we all know, Gabby, Scooter is an enthusiastic sniffer, but his eyesight seemed to be letting him down. He had a lot of trouble with the flowerbeds and got distracted by the kids next door bunging stuff over the fence at him. It was a different story in the second half, Gary. He came out all guns blazing and, once he'd locked on, there wasn't any stopping him. A little slight wobble at the end, when he just stood there shaking his head, but a great pick-up in the dying moments. All in all, though, I'd say this was not a champion's performance, Gabby. Erm, Gary. Erm..."

Lawro: "Flowerbed trouble"

Dogs piss on lampposts, right?

FETCH!

Elzie Crysler, Lost Dog

by ribs

The **Guardog**

Big Town's smuggest broadsheet

Giving you the WHOLE picture

SPIKEY
garden of fear 11

DOG BY NAME, CAT BY NATURE – EVIL HAS NO LIMITS
(except he's got territory near the chemical factory, so avoid that if you can)

"I thought I could take him but he gave me a right kicking…"
Roland from next door
"He nearly scratched my fricking eyes out, the bloody bastard…"
Patch from next door but one

STINKY BROS PRESENTS
An ARCHIE/ARCHIE PRODUCTION STANLEY FROM LONG LANE TRIXIE FROM THE VILLAS AND SPIKEY AS HIMSELF
"SPIKEY GARDEN OF FEAR 2"

BARKING BY SEAMUS FROM THE FLAT ABOVE THE POODLE PARLOUR
BASED ON HEARSAY AND URBAN FOLKLORE SPREAD BY THE CATS OF BIG TOWN

Suitable only for
dogs of 7 years
and over

X-BREED

Warning! Beware! There is a dangerous new type of dog prowling the streets of Big Town. This strange mutt's name is Lucky and he's what is known in the trade as a "cut and shut". This is where the front and back sections of two different dogs (often dogs written off in road accidents) are welded together by criminal gangs and passed off as a brand new animal. Although the resulting beast looks just like a normal dog, it's likely to fall in half when chasing a stick and cause a terrible to do.

GUILT TRIP

What has Simon the guilty spaniel been up to this month. Has he...

a) Done a big ploppie behind the television again?
b) Eaten the two lamb chops that were left out to defrost?
c) Torn to shreds his doting owner's finest Belgian lace sofa throw that she bought on a day-trip to Bruges in 1973?

Answers on a postcard to the usual address. The winning entry will receive a torn lace sofa throw and a swift kick up the arse.

MAN OF THE MONTH

After another month of furious in-fighting behind closed doors among the members of the self-appointed quango that has taken it upon itself to dish out these meaningless and divisive awards, we can announce this month's winner. For the 27th time in a row, *Bitch's* coveted Man of the Month award has gone to the resin-moulded figure that stands outside the butcher's on Big Town High Street. Rain or shine, he is always there, made out of fibre glass but uncannily realistic. In fact, he's so lifelike that there's a canine cult growing around him. The cult, known as The Comedy Butcher Cult, claim that the figure comes alive at night and hands out free sausages.

COMPETITION

WIN SOME MEAT!

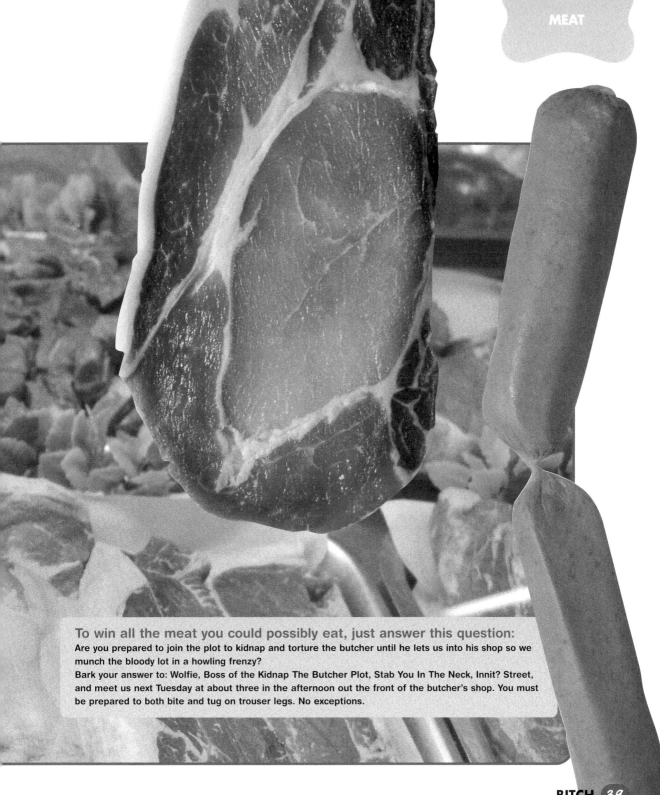

To win all the meat you could possibly eat, just answer this question:
Are you prepared to join the plot to kidnap and torture the butcher until he lets us into his shop so we munch the bloody lot in a howling frenzy?
Bark your answer to: Wolfie, Boss of the Kidnap The Butcher Plot, Stab You In The Neck, Innit? Street, and meet us next Tuesday at about three in the afternoon out the front of the butcher's shop. You must be prepared to both bite and tug on trouser legs. No exceptions.

FOOD & DRINK

THE PAVEMENT IS MY PLATE

Five top celebrity chefs tell us about their favourite "found" foods. It's a thrilling journey around the taste buds that will leave you slobbering as if Pavlov himself had left the buzzer on and gone down the pub

NIGELLA
"There's nothing I love more than a moist, creamy cone, stuffed roughly upside down in the sand at the beach. Its hard, pointing apex, straining heavenwards, is just begging for the attention of my warm mouth. I could lick one of those all day long."

JAMIE
"Awight, geezer! Once I've sorted out the grub that Big Town's pups get to eat, making sure it's all top gear what's nutritious and pukka and will help them grow up healthy, I like to munch on a rotten old kebab out the bin. Nice one!"

SENSUAL

PUKKA

COME ON

PISSED

FLOYD

"Bugger the bloody food, just give me a tin bowl filled to the brim with booze. I really don't care what it is – gin, vodka, whisky, Bacardi Breezer, meths, lighter fluid, anything. I'd even suck a cider flavoured lolly with all ants on it if I thought it'd get me pissed."

DELIA

"This really is an extremely simple dish to prepare. I like to call it Noodles Down The Drain and it always goes down well on a wet Saturday afternoon when Big Town are one-nil down to Other Town United. That's when we need a twelfth man, you see. Come on! Let's be 'avin' ya! Where are ya?!"

FUCK OFF

GORDON

"Call that a sandwich? You fucking useless wanker, you nearly fucking poisoned me. I'm going to puke up now, you fuck-stick wanking bollocks knob-end little prick! Get out of my fucking kitchen before I fucking cut you, you fucking fucker! Fuck off!"

KENNEL DOKTOR

**Are you a useless mongrel? Do you live in a hovel?
Then let the lovely Ann sort it all out for you!**

This is Freddie – his kennel needs a makeover and fast!

"Help me, Kennel Doktor! I have a handsome new kennel made of finest pine, but I can't seem to create the right atmosphere. Whatever I do, the kennel just has a kind of boring, show-home feel you'd expect to see in a featureless box in Other Town or somewhere equally tasteless and dull where the proles live. I'm looking for a spot of glamour in keeping with my hectic lifestyle as a perpetually barking dog that gets tethered to a pole in the garden by owners who are off working 10 hours a day in the media, invariably followed by lovely dinners on expense accounts in the evening, and have largely forgotten their responsibilities as dog owners."

Kennel Doktor says:

"Oh dear. You can see the trouble that Freddie is having. He ha[s] few nice pieces here and there – a large bone (1), a blue blank[et] with a pretty-but-masculine paw print on it which was purchas[ed] by his owners when he was just a pup and they still cared abou[t] having a dog (2), a handsome purple plastic bowl full of Bonios a tin of Pedigree Chum (4) and a slipper made from animal hid[e] in the processing plant down near the abattoir (5) – but there [is] no sense of home about this kennel. This isn't suitable for days [of] relentless howling and barking in his desperate loneliness, and [no] place at all to develop the psychological problems which will la[ter] deepen and make Freddie a risk to the local community's child[ren.] But I'm sure that I can help…"

BEFORE

Kennel Doktor works her magic

"Covering the big bone with old leaves and mud has certainly helped that nice little accessory come to life. Elsewhere, I've strewn lots of general rubbish around the kennel, mostly filth-encrusted old newspapers that I found in the bin. Shoving a Bonio in the tin of Chum and spreading the mushy food all over the shop has helped create an ambience of chaos and horror, while some more leaves and mud mixed in with the food in the plastic bowl has transformed this place from an awful old dump into a proper reeking shit-hole. That's much more fitting for a dog like Freddie. Here he will be able to dwell on the terrible misfortune of having such uncaring owners, and build up intense feelings of rage and resentment at his leisure."

AFTER

CAMPAIGN FOR

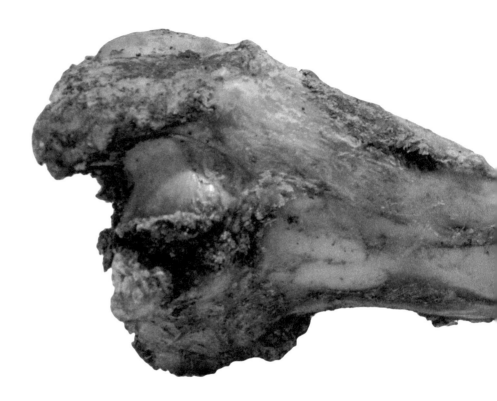

"I tried one of them rubber bones the other day and it were piss-poor"

Geoff Smith, 37 Main Street
(nothing to do with the CFRB, honest)

REAL BONES

Keeping it meaty!

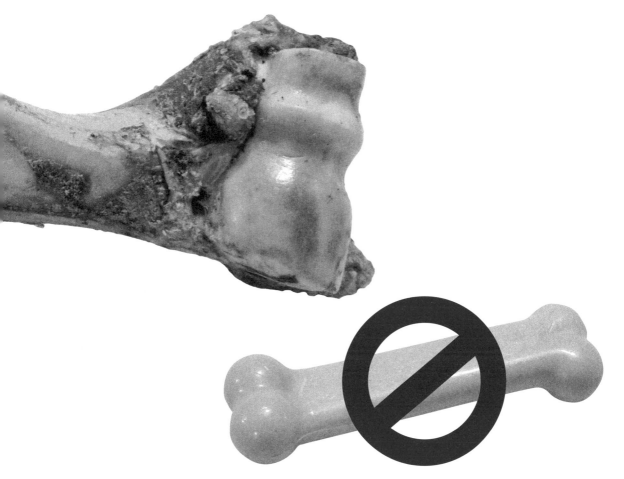

The CFRB is an independent consumer organisation. Membership is open to all dogs.
For more information about the CFRB, contact Geoff Smith at 37 Main Street

101
WAYS TO JOIN THE DOTS

Spot the dog. Yes, it's the black and white thing pictured right. But there's more to Spot than, erm, spots. He's one of the most famous dogs in Big Town…

You're one of the most famous dogs in Big Town, Spot, but you haven't always had an easy time of it, have you?
That's right. I haven't had what you'd call a dog's life. Well, I have had a dog's life, of course, because I'm a dog. But forgetting about that for a moment, I haven't had what you'd call a dog's life. If you see what I mean.

Quite. I understand that you had a traumatic experience as a puppy…
Yeah. I was dognapped when I was a few weeks old. A woman took me and a load of my brothers and sisters. She took 101 of us in total. Me, Dotty, Bingo, Lola, Trixie, Lassie, Titch, Billy… [*Five minutes later*] …Dozy, Beaky, Mick and Titch.

Erm, you said Titch twice.
Did I? Well, maybe there were only 100 of us, then. Me, Dotty, Bingo, Lola, Trixie, Lassie… ➔

And I think you'll find that Lassie's a collie, not a Dalmatian.
Oh, well, 101, 100, 99… I don't know. I'm a bit hazy about the details. It was very stressful. The woman who dognapped us turned out to be a right nasty piece of work. She'd only just got out of prison. She'd been done for boiling rabbits.

Glenn Close?
I'm not sure where it happened. It might have been Glenn Close. Or it could have been Acacia Avenue.

But at least you all managed to escape in the end, didn't you?
Yes, we did. Some of us appeared on *Blue Petra* after that. Which was my lucky break. For the next few years, I was on *Blue Petra* two or three times a week. I played the part of Shep. I spent most of my time hanging out with that bloke who used to jump out of aeroplanes. We were a great double act. Who could forget our famous catchphrase – "Get down, Shep"? Ah, happy days.

But that wasn't you, Spot. Shep was a collie, like Lassie. I've a feeling that Lassie might have played Shep, actually.
Oh, right. I'm so sorry. It's the trauma of the dognapping, you see. I sometimes get confused. Hmm, now I come to think of it, yes, you're right, that wasn't me. I was in that other programme instead. I was the star, you know. I had a fun time, being chased around by ghosts and monsters and stuff with Raggy, the →

smelly old hippy. They weren't real ghosts and monsters, mind. It was always just Uncle Festus dressed up. Hehehehehe.

Are you talking about Scooby Doo?

Uh-huh. Me and Raggy used to eat Scooby Snacks. Hehehehehe.

But you weren't Scooby Doo. Scooby was a Great Dane.

Oh heck. Well, what about the programme about the weird racing cars? I was in that with my old mate Dick Dastardly. We went on to do that thing with the pigeon. I can still remember some of my lines: "Sashen, rashen, frashen…"

Muttley? No, no, no, you weren't Muttley.

Ah, I know what I was in. The thing with that cat. What was his name? Blancmange? No, that's not right. Erm… Angel Delight? Arctic Roll? Erm… Ah, yes, Custard. That was it! Of course! Diddley-dee, diddley-dee, dee-dee-dee-dee-dee. Diddley-dee, diddley-dee, dee-dee-dee-dee-dee.

I'm sorry, Spot, but that wasn't you, either.

OK, I give up. What am I famous for, then?

You had a small part in *Macbeth*.

Shakespeare? I did Shakespeare? I don't recall that.

Yeah, you got under Lady Macbeth's feet just after she had murdered her husband. The bit where she says, "Out, out, damned Spot…" ●

THE POST

cocking up
since 1995

I SECOND THAT DEVOTION

We all love humans, but what is the best way for us to show our devotion to our best friends? And, of course, get free food for life

Humans: don't you just love them? Everything about them is great. Mainly, we love them because they feed us. But there's a lot more to it than that. There are the snacks, too, like Bonios and stuff. But what about all those other things? Like when they open tins of stinky food and spoon it into a bowl which they put on the kitchen floor where we can eat it. Isn't that great? It's not simply about food, though, is it? Sometimes, my owner gives me pieces of chocolate. And that's proof of how great people are. Isn't food great?

But if you're thinking the only reason we love humans so much is because they give us free food, think again.

When you need to take a shit, your owner will always be there, smiling and shouting "Walkies!" and dangling your lead in front of your nose. When you drop a coil in the corner behind the television, he or she will lovingly rub your nose in it and kick you up the arse. How great is that? It's totally great, actually. And if it wasn't for people, who'd throw all the sticks we love to chase? Name one other creature on the face of the planet that can throw sticks. Except monkeys. **->**

A devoted dog, yesterday

So, given that humans are the greatest things ever, how can we possibly repay them? Answer: with slavish devotion! It's a state that comes as naturally to us as hunting in packs, attacking badgers in a senseless battle to the death, or whimpering pathetically at the slightest hint of getting blamed for tearing apart the new sofa that was delivered by Habitat just last week.

But there are lots of ways to display your servility in this confusing modern world of ours, and it can sometimes be difficult for a puppy with his gonads still intact to make the right choices. For example, taking a bite out of that small human who drives your owner to distraction is not wise. You might think that you're defending your glorious leader, but you're actually attacking their young – and they don't take too kindly to that. Just ask Growler. You'll need a special dog ouija board if you want to talk to Growler, though, on account of him being a dead dog thanks to an injection administered by the vet. You know what we mean, don't you? Be careful, friends. It's a jungle out there.

To help you to navigate through the dizzying maze of choices for every devoted dog, we present a Top Trumps-style rip-out-and-chew guide to some of the human-serving jobs that you can think about doing while staring at your fantastic, wonderful, brilliant, terrific, sensational, amazing, all-round great person with quivering admiration as they get the tin opener out.

Hunting Hound

This one seems to split human opinion right down the middle. Some of them will dress up in red tunics and follow you around on horseback yelling "Tally-ho!" as you chase a fox across the fields with the intention of savagely tearing it limb from limb when you corner it. But others will shout "Oi! Bastards!" at you and throw aniseed all over the place, which makes your nose go mental. Too controversial by half, if you ask us. And also technically illegal.

Mountain Rescue Dog

A fabulous way to show your commitment to humans. Selflessly trudging through miles of snow to rescue a mountaineer in trouble, while cheering everyone with your endlessly positive demeanour, is guaranteed to earn you serious Brownie points and maybe a medal. Please note this position is only open to St Bernards and, due to new legislation from those mandarins in Europe, you have to supply your own barrel of booze. At least, that's what Kilroy in Acacia Avenue says.

Many are called, fancy trying to n find rememberin enough, so I wo of living long en for being blast lifetime to see tin can filled w will need a spe

TOP DO TRUMP

HOW TO PLAY THE

Come on, doggies! It's easy! Don't b have to read and that. Look at these pictures if you want – they should gi al idea), and choose a job that loo thing you could do. If you're really out the description and think abo would be if you did that job for you and whine until they feed you walkies. Then just forget all abo easy! It really is! It's a dog's life, a

Guide Dog

There are few gigs more worthy than this one. You're allowed into supermarkets and everybody loves you. They almost think that you're better than them. And in many ways, you are. It's bloody brilliant! The down side is that this job is normally restricted to Labradors who look both dependable and cute, even when they are dumping. It can be tough at the top – and some of us will never know what that feels like. But, hey, no worries, cos if there's one thing a dog always knows, it's his place!

e Dog

hosen. And I, for one, don't
controls of a rocket ship. I
the when I'm eating difficult
confident about my chances
ppreciate being appreciated
ace. Still, it's a chance of a
ad explodes when you fly in a
ydrogen. Just ask Laika. You
ouija board, though (etc).

Sniffer Dog

Got a decent nose for smack, crack, charlie, E, whizz, weed and/or PCP? Don't mind anti-social hours? Like airports? Keen on blue serge and an atmosphere of discipline and camaraderie? Then you would make an ideal rozzer's drug hound. The only trouble with this particular man-serving position is that people aren't always too happy about your sterling work, especially the skinny, twitchy ones who get banged to rights and end up having to do some serious stir. Whatever that means. Woof!

Greyfriars Bobby

Also known as Devotedly Sitting On Your Master's Grave Until You Grow Old And Die Yourself And They Build A Statue Of You And You Become More Famous Than Your Master Could Ever Have Possibly Hoped To Have Been (As Brilliant As He Was). Only one dog has attained this level of reciprocal worship. And his name was Greyfriars Bobby. Disney made a blockbuster film out of it and everything. Greyfriars Bobby now runs a successful ringtone company based in Miami.

cos you
just the
e gener-
e sort of
d, check
rilliant it
hen howl
you for
, it's *that*
!

Official Science Diagram* of a Great Human

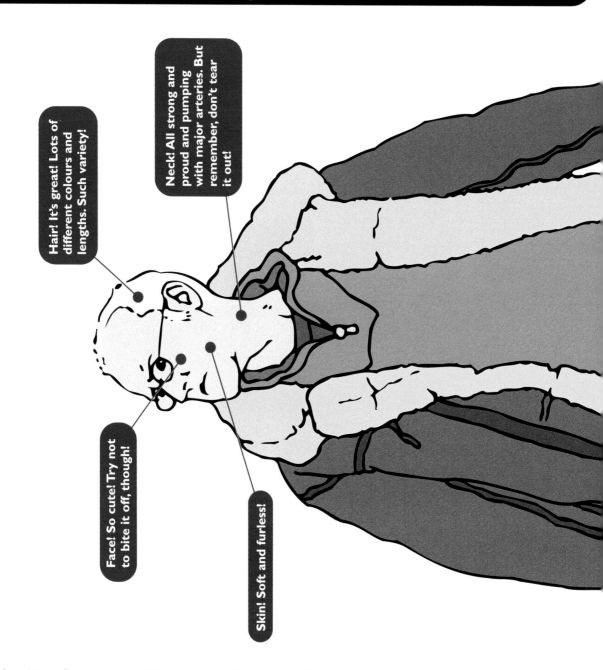

* Patch says it's proper official science and he should know cos his owner works in the chemists on Saturday mornings

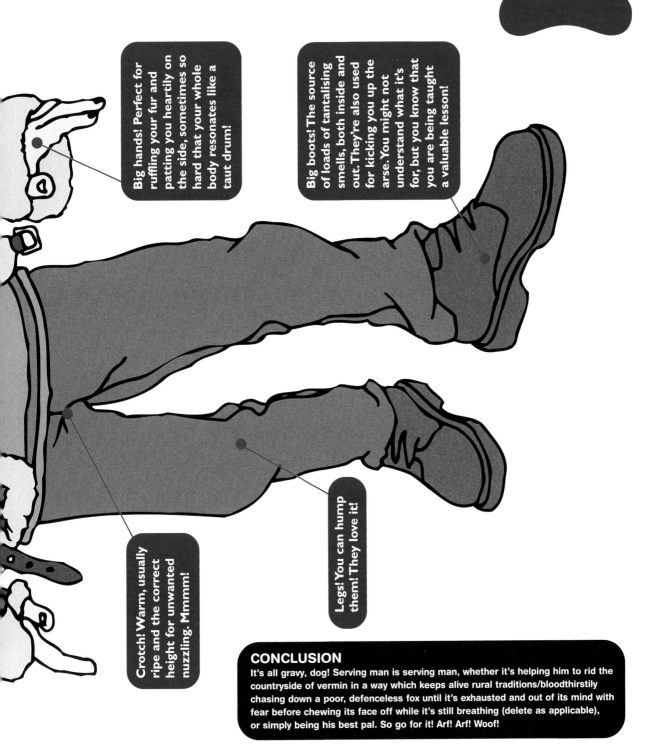

Big hands! Perfect for ruffling your fur and patting you heartily on the side, sometimes so hard that your whole body resonates like a taut drum!

Big boots! The source of loads of tantalising smells, both inside and out. They're also used for kicking you up the arse. You might not understand what it's for, but you know that you are being taught a valuable lesson!

Crotch! Warm, usually ripe and the correct height for unwanted nuzzling. Mmmm!

Legs! You can hump them! They love it!

CONCLUSION
It's all gravy, dog! Serving man is serving man, whether it's helping him to rid the countryside of vermin in a way which keeps alive rural traditions/bloodthirstily chasing down a poor, defenceless fox until it's exhausted and out of its mind with fear before chewing its face off while it's still breathing (delete as applicable), or simply being his best pal. So go for it! Arf! Arf! Woof!

SCRAPHEA

CHALLENGE

There are many stars in the doggy showbiz constellation, but only one of them is made out of metal – and his name is K-9. Our Entertainment correspondent Poppy tracked down the former screen idol whose amazing rags-to-riches-to-rags-again story should be a warning to every time-travelling robot dog in Big Town ->

K-9

I first sniffed out K-9 when rumours began circulating that the Big Town scrapheap had a brand new celebrity inhabitant. This was nothing unusual in itself; it was only last year that Pounder, the notorious human biter, endured a three-day siege at the heap after he'd escaped the vet's lethal injection and hidden in a Ford Fiesta. He was eventually caught by men wearing peaked caps who dragged him away in a big butterfly net and put him in the back of a van with bars on the window.

And who could forget the brief glimmer of glamour that the scrapheap enjoyed when Fifi LaTrix, then recently retired from her modelling career, got lost and wandered around the oil drums and rusty old cookers for several minutes before wizzing next to the pile of tyres and leaving?

But this new celeb dog was different, my sources told me. For starters, he'd arrived by way of the electro magnet and was made of special space metal. He'd not just served his master, the mysterious Dr Who, with

heart-warming devotion, he'd also saved the world and several other planets in the solar system and beyond, both in the past and the future, from certain destruction by evil forces made out of latex and thinly disguised household objects. Like toilet roll tubes and egg whisks. This dog had saved planets which hadn't been invented yet! This dog was, of course, K-9.

When I first found K-9, he was reluctant to reveal his identity. He tried to throw me off the scent by telling me his name was

Dougal. But I eventually won his trust and he started to reminisce about his days of fame and glory.

"Oh, it was marvellous," he intoned, robotically. "I had all the doggie treats and the high-grade 20/20 lubricant I could swallow, and my contract was very strict about me having my own dressing room, make-up girl and spot welder. I thought it was going to last forever."

K-9 shot to fame when he became Dr Who's companion during the late 1970s. He wasn't in any way a cheapskate attempt to cash in on the popularity of the robots in the fabulously popular *Star Wars* movie, even to the point of ripping off the voice of C-3PO. Indeed, such was K-9's admirable hard work on behalf of mankind that he even went off on an adventure of his very own and managed to foil a dastardly plot by a coven of witches (albeit with the help of Leela or Romana or the other one).

"I used my nose laser to dramatic effect in that piece. Everyone said that it was the finest nose laser work they'd ever seen."

Despite this, K-9 fell out of favour and gradually became less reliable, particularly during the events now known in legend as the 'Warrior's Gate' series.

"I was really abusing my electrodes," K-9 admitted to me in that smug, chirpy way of his. "It was getting more difficult for me to save the universe or even a planet. Even sorting out a bit of poxy old witchcraft in Gloucestershire took a whole hour. I was tired. And I only had 28k of RAM to keep the little red light blinking behind my eye visor thing and the ariel things sticking out my head spinning around. I was getting rusty. My performances were starting to suffer. Perhaps I corrected the Doctor once too often. Perhaps I shouldn't have said 'insufficient data' quite so many times."

And so K-9 found himself out of work and was evicted from the Tardis, the only place he had ever known as home.

"It was a lot bigger on the inside than the outside, you know," K-9 told me proudly. "But it was always breaking down. One time, the clutch went and we ended up in

Andromeda 16 in the 23rd Century, when everyone looked like Vikings with stupid cardboard suits on. I don't even want to talk about what happened when the timing belt snapped in that alternative universe where hairy blobs run Britain with an iron fist. Thankfully, the Brigadier came along and saved us in his Landrover."

Following his dramatic sacking from Dr Who's employ, K-9 eked out a living as a robber's dog and a bulldog chewing a wasp, before auditioning for the obscure 1980s underground rock band the Dog-Faced Hermans. But they were looking for a drummer, not a faulty mechanical mutt that leaked oil all over the stage.

K-9's final humiliation came when he briefly dallied in the cut-throat world of doggy fashion. "I quickly found out what was meant by 'do it doggy style', let me tell you…" he said, wincing with memories too painful to share.

"That was probably the lowest point," he continued, still talking with a sort of cheerful emotionlessness. "I'd hang **➡**

A DALEK REMEMBERS

Bitch caught up with Squadron Leader Dalek 13 (Ret'd), who was signing copies of his recently published *Exterminate! Amusing Anecdotes From 400 Years Of Trying To Wipe Out The Human Race* (Bantam Press, £9.99) at the Big Town bookshop. When we mentioned K-9, the much-respected Dalek warlord regaled us with stories of low-budget derring-do.

"Ha! Ha! Ha! Yes, I remember K-9. We eviscerated 40,000 of your bio-dogs in an attempt to discover the secret of K-9's awesome nose-laser. If you had a pet dog go missing between 1978 and 1982, chances are it was us that took it. But don't worry, we merely conducted a series of painful surgical procedures upon the hapless creatures. Without the use of anaesthetic. I shall never forget the stench of mortal canine fear that filled our Dalek Experiment Chambers during that time. It smelled like… victory. It was only then we discovered that bio-dogs don't have nose-lasers, and that K-9 was probably just made out of corrugated cardboard, old kitchen utensils and futuristic-looking bits of plastic. The nose-laser had been added by hand in post-production using a red felt-tip pen. It was more animation than fearsome death ray. Armed with this information, we were able to disregard the Doctor's little pet and impose a thousand-year Dalek Reich on the inhabitants of Axos which abides to this day. Do I get paid for this? I usually get £75 off Channel 5 for an interview…"

Substantial oil leak

Casually discarded cigarette

around petrol stations and lick the drips that came out of the nozzles after someone filled up with unleaded super. They were desperate times." So desperate, in fact, that K-9 viewed his new abode, the scrapheap, as a step up in the world. "You know, it's alright here, really," he told me. "You can keep your luxury dog space baskets and your time traveller kennels. For me, this is proper living. There's a sense of reality to being in the ghetto which reminds you of where you come from. Only the other day, for example, I was chewed for several hours by the scrapheap owner's Doberman. And that reminded me how I was constructed by Professor Marius in an environment-controlled space laboratory using the most advanced components and techniques of the 51st Century."

Despite his apparent enthusiasm for the heap, I could tell that K-9 still hankered for a life in the fast lane. "I've been waiting for a call from Celebrity Big Brother," he said. "They know how to contact me. I've got a fax machine built-in and they know that. Or Strictly Come Dancing. I'd even consider Fort Boyard – I'm not proud."

Pride is something K-9 can't afford. He keeps his memorabilia in a broken tumble dryer, his treasured possessions including faded photographs of him with various Dr Who assistants and a copy of the issue of *Mayfair* that featured well racy shots of Jo Grant all naked, her legs wrapped around a Dalek's sink plunger weapon thing like it was some kind of enormous man-phallus. It was while I was rifling through his private papers in typical journalistically-licensed intrusiveness that I came across a pay slip from his last employer – Bigtitbirds.com.

It turned out that K-9's awesome time-travelling processing power could only earn him money as a server for a porno website. Not an especially good one, at that. And when Apple launched OSX, he lost even that lowly gig.

But there was one final indignity, which conveniently took place just as I was trying to think of a way to end this article. As my photographer and I left the scrapheap, a passing human threw a burning cigarette close to the trail of fuel leaking from K-9's rear. We heard the explosion and rushed back to discover the former time-travelling automaton engulfed in flames.

We were too late to save him. ●

K9 OBITUARY

Since the tragic demise of K-9, tributes have been flooding in from across the known (and unknown) universe. Robot 537268927363 (Rev. 5.6), better known as Eric (pictured above), was one of a tiny handful of poorly-constructed props for children's television programmes of the 1970s who kept in touch.

"I remember that we travelled many galaxies and had lots of super adventures together. One time, the Doctor left him tied up outside this supermarket in the Nebula Cluster. He left him there for 3,000 years. When we went back to get him, he was all covered in rust. It took six tins of Hammerite to bring him back to his former glory. I'll miss him. Do I get paid for this? I usually get £2.50 off Channel Five…"

WHY CAN'T WE

ISSUED BY THE BIG TOWN CANINE/FELINE LOVE ASSOCIATION – FIGHTING PREJUDICE AND PRO

JUST GET ON ?

HARMONY AND EQUALITY IN NON-SPECIES SPECIFIC RELATIONSHIPS (EXCEPT HAMSTERS)

ON THE BALL ⚽
FRUITY

She's married to Striker, Big Town's legendary canine footballer, and shagging most of his team-mates. In an exclusive interview, Fruity talks frankly about her rampant sexual appetite

Thanks for inviting us into your kennel, Fruity. The decor is intriguing. The photo above the fireplace is very, erm, explicit. Is that really you and your husband Striker having sex?

Yeah. It's lovely, innit? One newspaper said I had "truly appalling taste". That's lovely, innit? I was chuffed about that. There's more photos of me at it in the bog. Do you want to see them?

Not especially. To be honest, we're not the least bit interested in you. We're only talking to you because you're married to a famous footballer.

Aww, that's lovely of you to say so. I used to have my own career as a howler, of course. That was how Striker and I met, you know. Strikes – that's my pet name for Striker – was running around the football pitch, pushing the ball with his nose and yapping like a lunatic as he was chased by a bunch of angry humans in muddy shorts, and I was standing on the sidelines howling, "Stri-ker! Striii-ker! Striiiii-ker!! Striiiiiiiiiiii…" ➜

Yes, yes, we get the picture.
Anyway, Strikes and I had a bowl of water together after the game and that was that. I was attracted to him cos of his lovely golden balls. He was attracted to me cos of my lovely howling and also cos I'm a lot more posh than what he is.

You've been seen out with one or two other footballers, though, haven't you? Scorer, for instance.
Scorer? Well, erm, yeah, that's true. Scores – that's my pet name for him – did score with me. Hahaha. Scores scored with me, geddit? Hahaha. That's funny, innit? But that's what happens when you're a footballer's wife, you know. I spend all my time bitching about the other girls and getting off with their dogs.

So are the rumours about you and Kicker true, then?
Me and Kicks? Yeah, they're true. Kicks is lovely, you know.

And you and Header?
Me and Heads? Yeah, him an' all.

And you and Becker?

Becks? Nah, there's no truth in that. Anyhow, I think you'll find that Becker is a tennis player not a footballer.

What about you and Stan Collie?

Aww, yeah, Stan's lovely. He took me out dogging, you know. That was lovely. All that running around and barking…

Right, well, shall we talk a bit more about your kennel?

Nah, who cares about that guff? How about a shag instead?

Erm, I really should ask you about soft furnishings…

Sod that. You're lovely, you are. And I'm well up for it, you know. I'll look out the window to make sure the old man ain't coming home from training early and you do me from behind… ●

GO LIKE TH

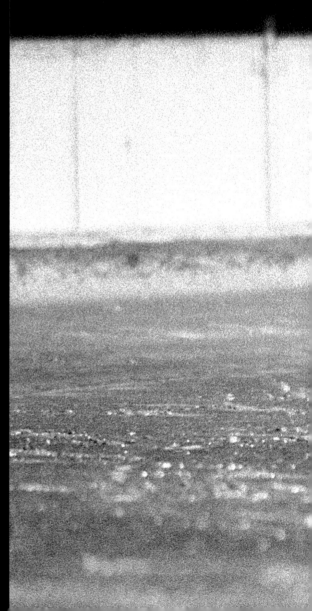

When our Racing And Hard Dogs Generally correspondent Breathless Dawson told us that a local boy was looking like he could be a true contender in the tough world of greyhound racing, we dispatched him to write a perceptive profile which would give us an unflinching insight into the dog-eat-dog world of the very hardest of all sports. Instead, Breathless Dawson sent us the following confused gibberish ➔

It is only once in a generation that a dog comes along who can run like this boy. He has everything; pace, build, temperament and a large lolling tongue that dangles out of his mouth nearly all the time. He whimpers like no other and his pathetic quivering skills are a wonder to behold.

The dog I am talking about is called Jarvis La Motta, known as Jake to his mates, and he lives at the smelly house down by the Big Town docks. You know, Number 38 Rough Bollocks Road. It's off Stab You In The Neck, Innit? Street, opposite the Duff You Up Arms pub. Jake's already won the Golden Nutsack (For Running Like The Clappers) Award three times and his fearless will to win in the harsh world of Monday night greyhound race meetings in the middle of winter has earned him the nickname Twinkle Toes.

Getting near this amazing dog for an interview is not easy. He is surrounded by an army of minders, all old friends of his from the 'hood, and they make it very difficult to approach him. But luckily, I know his brother, Joe 'Pesky' La Motta.

Joe is a failed racer. Since his career stalled in the blocks, he's been running an illegal gambling den. He's as mad as a box of monkeys, but he promised to get me close to Jake.

"Before Jake got into the racing game," Joe told me as we sat in his seedy apartment between the gasworks and the big Sainsbury's (the one with the car wash) on Big Town's Lower East Side, "he was just a drifter, a bum, a no-good sonomabitch."

According to Joe, Jake was once a butcher's dog. As an alienated and emotionally dislocated veteran of the Big Fight (the four-day battle of attrition which only ended when the Big Town Bruisers were forced to withdraw in ignominy and defeat), it was the only job he could get. He'd work the shifts that none of the other mutts would take and go to the run-down neighbourhoods that the other butchers' dogs would avoid. Jake didn't care. He'd even go into cat districts after dark, running alongside the butcher's old-fashioned bicycle (like that one Granville had in *Open All Hours*), despising yet wallowing in the seamy underbelly of Big Town.

"It reached a climactic and cataclysmic climax when Jake started looking in a mirror and saying, 'You barking at me?' over and over again," explained Joe. "It was after that he went nuts in the rabbit hutch at Number 54 Scary Street in the Bowery near the East River and scoffed four bunnies. There was a lot of blood. On the upside, though, he didn't need to eat for three days."

Jake's commitment to his craft has a dark side, then. Behind the façade of a successful sportsdog lurks a tortured psyche which can cause him to fly into a jealous rage at the slightest provocation or imagined insult.

"There was this one time when we had a bad confrontation, me and him," continued Joe, who was by now dishing the dirt ➡

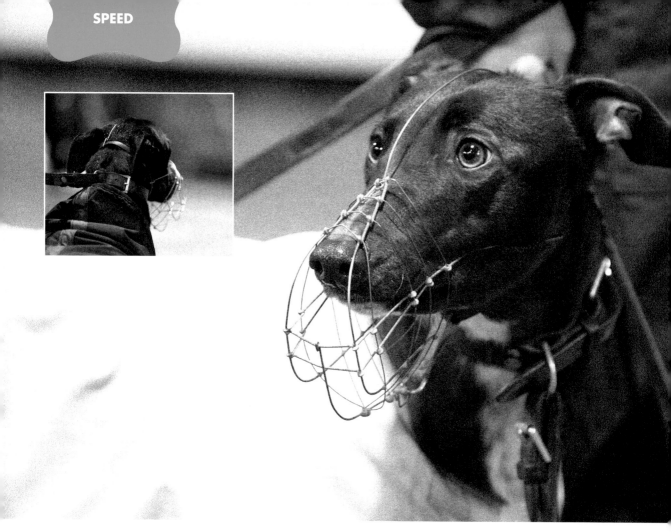

like so many spilled beans on his psycho brother that he reminded me of some sort of singing canary. "It was all because of a dame. Her name was Vicki. She was a high-class broad. I remember she kicked up a stink of merry hell when she found out the restaurant down at the track didn't serve Caesar Chicken in Mediterranean Sauce with Goujons of Truffle and Shaved Parmesan Flakes. She was real hungry, so she ate what they normally serve down there. When she discovered it was mechanically recovered horse spinal cord and asshole meat, she collapsed. She needed several weeks of intense pampering over at the Big Town Poodle Parlour in order to recover.

"Anyhow, Jake got this idea that me and her had been, well, you know… He was crazy with jealousy. He kept saying, 'Did you fuck my wife?' in a really threatening way, over and over, pronouncing it with a slightly different emphasis each time. But I got my own back by saying, 'How am I funny? Like a clown? What is so funny about me? What the FUCK is so funny about me? Tell me. Tell me what is so funny,' in an even more threatening way. That put the willies right up him. Then I shot him in the foot."

As fascinating as these tales of sibling squabbling were, I wanted to see Jake in action. The next night, I went to the races.

Witnessing this 65-pound heavyweight superstar tear up the sand track like some kind of really fast, erm, running dog, chasing an old bit of bin bag round and round as if it was a rabbit, his long tongue flapping out of his gaping gob with all dribble coming off it, was going to be a sporting event to remember.

Unfortunately, Jake came fourth out of four, mainly because he spotted someone eating a beefburger at the first bend and became disoriented, stopped running, and sat down to sniff his backside and give his balls a thorough lick. Moments later, he announced that he was quitting racing. It was a sad end to a stellar career which had seen him net more than 300 Bonios in prizes. **->**

THE CANA-SUTRA

This classic ancient masterpiece covers all the classic positions from doggy style to doggy style

CAUTION: POSITION MAY CAUSE "LOCKING"

Jake's descent into a hell of his own making was rapid, but his brother Joe wasn't blameless. There have been suggestions that Joe told Jake to throw his final race, because a huge stack of cash had been placed on him at the bookies and they could win big if they bet the other way. That night, Jake was overheard talking to Joe in the back of a cab as they left the waterfront for good. "I coulda had class," Jake was saying. "I coulda been a contender. I coulda been somebody, instead of a bum which is what I am."

But we shouldn't think of the bloated figure of the failed racer when we speak of Jarvis "Jake" La Motta. Let us instead remember that wiry frame stretched full length, his muscular body propelling him around the track on a dreary and wet Monday night for the enjoyment of several dozen pie-eating humans who are also keen on scratch cards and bingo.

In the words of Joe "Pesky" La Motta: "You fucking shit-kicking, horse-manure-smelling motherfucker, you!" ●

MUDDY WATERS
HEALTH RESORT

Big Town's Premier Spa

Treatments include pepto-rhinocide googleflaxology (with rejuvenating* colonic aquasphere knob squirt of judderphosphate nucleids) and, of course, our famous patented ghastly stinking fetid water with green scumoids and old fag ends (above)

Our commitment to you:
"You will never be this filthy again. Or quite as riddled with disease**"

MUDDY WATERS HEALTH RESORT, BIG TOWN SEWAGE TREATMENT PLANT, NEAR THE GASWORKS AND THE POISONOUS CHEMICAL FACTORY
Cost for a two-day visit: six bones. Three-day visit: four bones

*If, by rejuvenating, you mean "will probably cause death from a hideous respiratory disease", that is
**Infection with e-Coli optional, tapeworm infestation guaranteed!!!

THE TURDER PRIZE

There's nothing like a really good crap. Except when it comes to the annual Turder Prize, which always guarantees a heated debate on the very concept of shit and its place in the modern world. We've had two decades of controversy – and this year's event looks like being no exception ➔

Since its inception in 1984, when the awards ceremony took place in the parky's hut at the Recreation Ground, the Turder Prize has courted controversy. The first shortlist of nominations caused uproar in Big Town. Eddie, the boot-faced Labrador from Main Street, was livid when the new competition was announced.

"The very idea you can grade turds and then say one turd is somehow *better* than another is obscene," he railed. "You simply can't quantify shit like that. Who are these mandarins that have set themselves up as arbiters of taste, anyway?" And to prove his point, he bit the postman.

Lord Feathers

If the very idea of a prize for shit caused trouble from the start, the public row that greeted its launch was nothing compared to the furore when Desmond from the Big Town Dogs' Home won the competition in 1989 with his bizarre entry, *A Very Badly Chewed Rubber Bone*.

"They Call This SHIT?!!" screeched the front page of the Big Town Evening News. An editorial by the newspaper's editor, Lord Feathers, summed up the sense of outrage felt among Big Town's establishment: "When some insolent young pup comes along and tries to pass off a very badly chewed rubber bone as a piece of shit, well, that's just the limit. But then to be given a prize for such twaddle? Where will it end? With cats being allowed to enter? This is political correctness gone mad!"

The Turder Prize continued to be in the eye of the storm following allegations that the 1990 winner, Pip, didn't actually create his entry. Pip angrily dismissed claims that *Look At My Enormous Poo* was actually the work of a German Shepherd called Jonty. "I'm not the Milli Vanilli of the shit world. That grunty was all mine," he barked at his critics when he collected his prize of a stick and a stinky old tennis ball.

This year, like every year, an angry mob of mental cases gathered outside the offices of the Turder Prize Selection Committee to stage a protest. "Most of the stuff in the competition is complete rubbish," snarled Joe the mongrel, a nutbag who gets angry at anything with the slightest provocation. "Honestly, my little three-week-old puppy could do a better ploppie than any of that bloody lot," he added. "All these so-called artists make me sick." And in one of this year's more ironic twists, the entry hotly tipped to scoop the prize is actually called *My Three-Week-Old Puppy Did This*.

We tracked down Piper & Drummer, the avant-garde duo responsible for *My Three-Week-Old Puppy Did This*, and

Drummer, yesterday

Piper & Drummer, last year

probed them about the inspiraton for their fascinating piece.

"We asked ourselves some very searching questions about the purpose of our work," they explained. "We investigated our own motivations and looked carefully at what turds meant for us. Then we got Binky, our three-week-old puppy, to drop one onto a canvas, stuck it inside an old frame we had lying around and slapped a price tag of a million Bonios on it. Marvellous."

My Three-Week-Old Puppy Did This has already been sold to Charles Chachi (the one-time star of *Happy Days* and the single most important collector behind the Big Town shit art movement). It was Charles Chachi's purchase of Damien Omen's *Shit Cut In Half In A Glass Tank* for 100,000 Bonios during the late 1990s that sparked what the style magazines have dubbed the BigArt revolution. ➤

Perhaps the most famous Turder Prize winner of all time, Randy's screen-printed *Poo Variations* defined not only an era of shit, but set the tone for the entire decade in which it was created. It's a piece which still resonates to this day. As Randy himself said: "Uh, it was easy for me to make poo into an, uh, icon. It's like, uh, totally what it is already. One day, all poo will be famous for like, uh, 15 minutes. Totally."

Another entry enraging critics this year is *White Poo*, a video installation by Rover The Second. His controversial 15-minute film is a time-lapse piece which charts the slow metamorphosis of a turd from a fresh, conker-brown bum sausage to a crumbling, chalky white, ghost-like poo. Rover The Second claims that his work "tackles ideas of mortality" and also answers the age-old question, why don't we see white dog shit these days? "It's because the streets actually get cleaned these days," says Rover. "It's not the 1970s, when the country was going to hell in a handcart, you know."

There's strong opposition to Rover The Second's work on both sides of the divide. Insiders claim that, by using video, Rover is divorcing shit lovers from the process of creation, because the screen acts as a barrier between the authenticity of the piece and those who view it. Big Town's tabloid press are also attacking *White Poo*, saying that, if you are going to present a video of a lump of shit and call it art, why not go the whole hog? Why not stick a candle on it and call it a birthday cake?

"Funnily enough, I'm currently working on a triptych which I am calling *White Poo Birthday Cake With A Candle On It*," says Rover The Second. "I think it's going to be a huge triumph." ●

White Poo – an abomination or a work of genius?

THE TURDER TIMELINE

Rex's *Turdus* (1987), made entirely in Latin, caused a fight on the recreation ground.

Ooh, I Think You'd Better Get Me To The Vet Quick (1993) was considered the weakest entry for a million years, but won the prize anyway. The resulting fight on the recreation ground lasted four days with no clear victor emerging.

The first Turder Prize was awarded to Terry's *My Big Dump* in 1984.

When Spike entered his biscuit-encrusted coil, *Fat Rush Nuts* (1990), three judges fainted.

Poo And Wazz (1998), a startling collage of mixed media broke with convention and started another fight on the rec. Boxer lost an ear.

1984...........................1990...........................1995...........................2C

OTHER TURDER WORKS

As well as Piper & Drummer and Rover The Second, there are lots of big-name BigArt shitters vying for this year's prize. Here's the best of the rest up for consideration...

They Pushed My Nose In It
This emotionally charged work recalls a puppyhood of awful abuse for its young creator, Lil' Doggie. Against all odds, Lil' Doggie has overcome his traumatic background and now ranks as one of the most promising poo talents in Big Town.

The Big Squeeze
Turder Prize veteran Johann has used humour to celebrate the honest toil involved in dropping the kids off at the pool.

Loaf
Simple lines and austere architecture have always marked out Lenny's work. *Loaf* is no exception. Remarkably, it also does actually resemble a small unsliced wholemeal.

Gruntus Maximus
With a cheeky nod to Rex's 1987 winner, the memorable *Turdus*, Lady's *Gruntus Maximus* is inspired by "films about gladiators".

(I Can't Get Me No) Satisfaction
Mick and Keef collaborated on this ode (or rather "ordure") to tension, but unfortunately Keef scoffed it before the judges saw it. It was, we're assured, "very impressive indeed".

Ooh, That's Better
A response to Mick and Keef's somewhat constipated effort, Basil's flat pancake is considered too moist by most observers.

Sniff It (Sniff It Good)
Pammy's entry this year focuses on pong rather than form and has, not surprisingly, divided the critics. Is this a new direction for shit or just a dead end?

Bum Plums
Don't be fooled by Herman's creation. It may look like a bowl of fruit sitting on a table, but there's a lot more to this than meets the eye. And that long, bendy shape is definitely not a banana.

Dave's *Surely That's Not Natural* (2004) turned out to be plastic. The cancellation of the fight on the rec caused a fight on the rec.

This year's entries are widely thought to be "rubbish".

TODAY

We Three ~~Kings~~ Queens

With pedigrees as long as a Great Dane's arm, these three King Charles Spaniels aren't known as the 'It Bitches' for nothing. But is there more to the famous Zog-Smartypants bloodline than meets the eye?

Thank you for agreeing to this interview. I'd like to ask…
Lady Rosemary Smartypants Uffington III: Now, before you go any further, I want to make it absolutely clear that we're not going to talk about the so-called "Loyal Family". Damned Corgis.
Mizz Tara Farmer Palmer Zog-Smartypants: Well said, mama.
Mizz Prunella Round The Twist Of Lemon Cheesecake To Go Zog-Smartypants: Yes, well said, mama. Damned upstarts. ➡

Mizz Tara: They're not even English. Damned Corgis are damned Welsh, aren't they?

Mizz Prunella: Welsh? Really? I thought they were German. Or is that Dachshunds?

Lady Rosemary: Welsh, German, whatever they are, those Corgis are no-good Johnny Foreigners and they shouldn't be called "the Loyal Family". That title is rightfully ours, you know. My beloved husband, the late Lord Double Brandy What-What Of Zog, must be spinning in his grave…

Mizz Prunella: Except he's not dead, mama. He ran orff with Fifi the maid, remember?

Mizz Tara: Sssssh!

Lady Rosemary *[gritting her teeth]*: Fifi La Trix! What did he see in her? Oh, the shame of it. What kind of a pedigree did that French bitch have? Poodles? Pah! I hate them.

Stupid woolly dogs. Just one step up from sheep. Poodles really are awful specimens, you know. If I ever see Fifi La Trix again, I shall bite her flicky little tail orff. Slut! Whore! Harlot! Grrrr!

Mizz Tara: Mama!

Erm, right, well, perhaps we'd better move on…

Lady Rosemary *[clearing her throat and smiling broadly at the interviewer]*: I'm so sorry about that. Anyway, as I was saying, my beloved Lord Double Brandy What-What Of Zog, who couldn't have run orff with Fifi the maid because he died in a tragic accident while out hunting pheasants with my brother, Sir Fotheringay Ra-Ra-Ra Rugger Bugger Smartypants Uffington, would be terribly upset if he knew that the proud Zog-Smartypants line had been usurped. We are the true blue bloods of Big Town, not those damned Corgis. **->**

Carpeton®

Embarrassing itching?
Burning anus?
Use Carpeton – it's strangely exciting!

Mizz Tara: Well said, mama. Orff with their heads!
Right, well, let's press on. As it happens, I didn't actually want to talk about the Loyal Family…
Mizz Prunella: THE LOYAL FAMILY?! How dare you mention them! Mama has already told you that she does not wish to speak about them. It'll be orff with your head, too, if you're not careful.
Lady Rosemary: Upstarts! Usurpers! Foreigners! Grrrrr!
Mizz Prunella *[to interviewer]*: See what you've done now.
Mizz Tara: You mustn't upset yourself like this, mama.

Lady Rosemary: Immigrants! Inbreeds! Bastards! Grrrrr!
Mizz Tara *[to interviewer]*: You'd better change the subject. Ask another question and make it quick.
Erm, right…Lady Rosemary, you recently won the Big Town Flower Show with your roses. What made you…
Mizz Prunella: Maid!? MAID!!!? How dare you mention Fifi La Trix. How did you know about her, anyway?
Lady Rosemary *[frothing at the mouth]*: HARLOT! HARLOT! HARLOT! GRRRRR!!! **➔**

Dad Not Back From The Vet's Yet?

THE DOG OUIJA BOARD COMPANY
Creators of fine dog ouija boards since 1973

For all your dead dog contacting needs

Pictured: The Sun And Moon special edition* made from a million anodised Bonios infused with vintage dog whiff. Gold-plated and saliva-proof. Actual ouija boards may differ in quality and, in all likelihood, will be rubbish.

Feeding pussies since 1953

www.k9charlatan.co.dog

Mizz Tara *[to Mizz Prunella]*: You'd better find the Bob Martin dog pills, Pru. Mama has really lost it this time.

Mizz Prunella fetches a packet of Bob Martin's and gives Lady Rosemary a tablet. Two minutes later…

Lady Rosemary: Now, where was I? Ah yes, Lord Double Brandy What-What Of Zog…He was a stupid old fool, you know. Not that I cared. I was far too busy getting rogered by Sir Fotheringay Ra-Ra-Ra Rugger Bugger Smartypants Uffington.

Mizz Tara: But Uncle Fotheringay is your brother, mama!

Lady Rosemary: Yes, dear. And he's also your father.

Mizz Prunella and Mizz Tara *[together]*: MAMA!!! ●

SPORT

A CLASSY HANG-JOB

Hanging onto things with a vice-like grip tends to be a small dog sport and has often been dismissed as "stupid" and "not really a sport at all". Tell that to Jack "Jack" Russell, this year's champion hanger-on, who takes us through the top hanging moves

"This is what's known as the Horse Tail Hang. It's a risky procedure, but it can be rewarded with speeds of up to 40 miles an hour. Make sure you don't hang on to the tail of a horse in a fox hunt or one that's going over the jumps in a steeple chase. They are both likely to end in injury and one is illegal."

"Here's a slight variation on the hanging theme. As such, it's a bit controversial. Notice how the hanger has managed to get his entire body through a tyre which is dangling from the tree and is hanging there, barking at his mates down below. The last dog to attempt this eventually died from starvation while hanging."

"This is an excellent example of how hanging can enhance your daily life. One of these two dogs (the one on the right) has been in training for months. Which do you think is going to win the tug-of-war and get to gorge on sossiges until he pukes?"

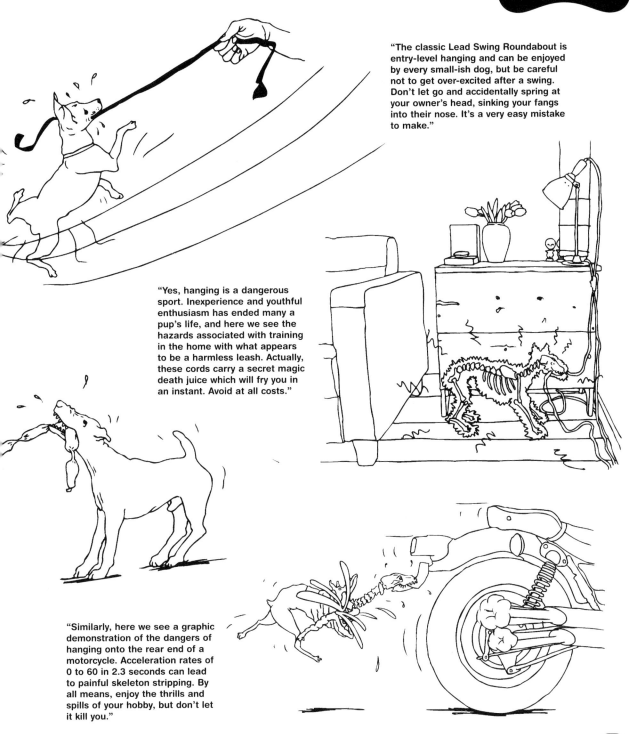

"The classic Lead Swing Roundabout is entry-level hanging and can be enjoyed by every small-ish dog, but be careful not to get over-excited after a swing. Don't let go and accidentally spring at your owner's head, sinking your fangs into their nose. It's a very easy mistake to make."

"Yes, hanging is a dangerous sport. Inexperience and youthful enthusiasm has ended many a pup's life, and here we see the hazards associated with training in the home with what appears to be a harmless leash. Actually, these cords carry a secret magic death juice which will fry you in an instant. Avoid at all costs."

"Similarly, here we see a graphic demonstration of the dangers of hanging onto the rear end of a motorcycle. Acceleration rates of 0 to 60 in 2.3 seconds can lead to painful skeleton stripping. By all means, enjoy the thrills and spills of your hobby, but don't let it kill you."

SNOW JOKE

Shocking horror at the Winter Olympics shocker

Snowflake Catching is always one of the most spectacular events at the Winter Olympics. It's one of the most popular, too. Dogs flock from the four corners of Big Town to marvel at the acrobatic leaps and the expert tongue flicking. In recent times, the crowd favourite has been Bob, the super-fit black pooch dubbed "The Canine Coiled Spring". Bob has held the Snowflake Catching title since 2001 and has regularly scored marks of 9.8 and 9.9, even from notoriously tough judges like Mac, the bad-tempered Highland Terrier.

We are sad to report, however, that Bob's phenomenally successful career appears to be over after a freak accident

Bob, just seconds before calamity

in this year's semi-finals which has left him tragically traumatised. He didn't get out of bed for a week. Not even for a choccie biscuit. A proper milk choccie biscuit at that, made by Cadbury's and everything, not something you'd find in the "Treats" section at the pet shop. They ought to do that place under the Trade Descriptions Act, if you ask us. Let's face it, as nice as they are, those waxy-tasting drops aren't really "treats", are they? They're not a patch on Maltesers or Smarties or Mini Eggs or Revels (not including toffee Revels, mind, because they get jammed up in your back teeth). Or Opal Fruits, which aren't even choccies and get jammed up in your back

teeth just like toffee Revels but are dead yummy all the same.

Sorry, we seem to have got distracted there. Where were we? Hmmm. Oh, yes, Bob. Well, although Bob is up and about now, he's still a bit wobbly. Details of what happened remain sketchy, but it's thought he was hit by the biggest ever snowflake to ever fall in the world ever. One minute he was getting ready for his famous triple twist and tuck (with pike) and the next he was spread-eagled on the ground, two parts snow to one part dog. The crowd initially roared with laughter, but it soon became clear that this was no joke. "This is no joke," shouted Bob's trainer, Gnasher

O'Grady, as he helped the dazed mutt to climb shakily to his feet.

The nasty bump on Bob's head is going down, but the mental scars won't be so quick to heal. Despite Gnasher O'Grady insisting that "the lad will be back in the fray next season", an anonymous source close to Bob (his next door neighbour Goldie) claims he's thinking about taking early retirement. To make matters worse, Bob has a permanently sore nose because he keeps glancing up at the sky and, as a result of not looking where he's going, is forever banging into lamp posts and trees. He's also taken to shouting "Avalanche!" every couple of minutes.

The biggest snowflake in the world appears

The moment of impact – and Bob's snowed under

BIG TOWN'S 25th ANNUAL DROOLING CHAMPIONSHIP

Slobber!!! Yee-haw!!! As you all know, the 25th Annual Drooling Championship took place last Thursday afternoon round the back of the library. And what a fabulous event it was, too. We haven't seen so much saliva since Pickles got locked inside the lorry that delivers tins of Pedigree Chum to the supermarket.

As always, the competition stayed true to the formula established a quarter of a century ago by Pierre the leaky-mouthed French dog, with three qualifying heats: Drooling *Au Naturel*, Assisted Drooling *Méthode Une (Avec Le Rubber Ball Stuffed In La Bouche)* and Assisted Drooling *Méthode Deux (Avec Le Unopened Packet Of Bonios Sur La Table)*. As usual, the winners of the heats then went head-to-head-to-head in a three-way tussle for the so-called Golden Tongue (a lump of wood once chewed by Pierre himself). As ever, it was a dramatic contest. By the end of it, the front row of spectators were drenched in dribble and looked like extras from the recent punk rock version of that classic canine musical *Howling In The Rain*.

This year's title was won by Bessie, the old hound with the squinty eyes and the weird teeth, who produced a grand total of 1.36 litres of top-notch slobber in the final. Our main picture shows Bessie at the saliva measuring bowl with one eye on the Bonios. Or perhaps both eyes. We're not altogether sure, to tell you the truth.

STIX

YOU WANT 'EM... WE FETCH 'EM

PROVIDING STICKS FOR BIG TOWN'S CANINES SINCE THE BEGINNING OF TIME

Our current range:

L'Organique
Selected for its unique shape and extra lichen

The Fat Boy
For the very, very, very large-gobbed indeed

La Longue
For the dog who prefers a longer stick but with girth, too

Le Classique (Extended)
Provides absurd but handleable length

The Surrey
A sturdy stick of sensible dimension for good dogs

The Chubster
For those looking to extend their bite and drool

The Twat
A tiny stick for a dog so small as to hardly count as a dog

Trading address: The Woods, Big Town. Actual sticks may differ in almost every way from examples shown

MOTORING

REX WRECKS!

All cars can be ruined by us dogs, but which ones are the most fun to pull apart? This month, the legendary Rex sets about a red one in fine style

When George from next door asked me if I wanted to sit in the passenger seat of his owner's new 4x4 and stick my head out of the window so that the rushing air filled my jowls and made them puff out like big, meaty, slobbery balloons, I leapt at the chance. After all, it isn't every day you get to make a nice new car stink of dog. It's a great way to accelerate its depreciation. This particular vehicle cost more than 30 grand, but I was determined it wouldn't be worth anything by the time I'd finished with it. ➜

Look at my meaty balloons

I was looking forward to shedding tons of my hair on the seats and drooling all over the dashboard. Plus I was busting for a waz and, if you're going to waz anywhere, you might as well do it on the fresh upholstery of a brand new car. Especially if it belongs to George's owners. Serves them right for driving a petrol-guzzling 4x4 just to pick the children up from school and go shopping at Waitrose. The bourgeois sods don't even live in the country.

My first impressions were good. If this car had been a bone, it would have been a large one and it would have sat up and said, "Eat me, big boy" in a squeaky voice, just like my favourite rubber toy. The Wankel Spunkel engine, with its overhead nosh pots and 15-valve gherkin radiator splodge, roared like a hog with a poker up its jacksie, and was capable of achieving a remarkable 10mph

in an ear wax vibrating five minutes. If it was going downhill and George had given us a push, that is.

I found that tearing at the soft upholstery with my fearsome gnashers quickly penetrated the faux-leather covers and revealed the cheap, bright yellow foam underneath. Another plus point for me was the discovery that, if anybody approached the vehicle, I could hurl myself at the windows and bark ferociously at them for ages and ages, spraying vast quantities of frothy spittle all over the interior in the process.

Thanks to the soaring temperatures outside and the fact that George had forgotten to leave a gap at the top of the window, I soon lost consciousness. Had the car not swerved out of control and gone over the edge of the Big Town cliff, landing on the beach and shattering the windscreen so I was able to escape from the jumble of twisted metal, I'd probably have ended up just another doggy statistic. When will you fools learn the sad truth that dogs die in hot cars?

All in all, I managed to reduce the on-the-road value of the car to approximately zero in not much more than 30 seconds – and I didn't even have to stink it out first by going for walkies in a field of moist cow pats, rolling around in them, and then leaping in the back seat before anybody could stop me. I really am brilliant at wrecking stuff, me.

Catch up with me again next month when my anti-social and out-of-control behaviour reduces the value of Eric's owners' new house by 50 per cent within 24 hours.

Rex and George: perfectionists

Car ruined, dog safe – mission accomplished

TRAVEL TIPS

No.17

ROMAN SHOWERS – THEY'RE FUN AND THEY'RE TASTY

Some call it gaffing up. Others call it yagging. It's also known as spewking, puking, oiping, upping, techicolor yawning and making a pavement pizza. Today, our favourite term is a Roman shower. But whatever you call it, there's nothing like a 100-mile round trip to your owner's relatives over a long bank holiday weekend to indulge in it. It is the sport of kings.

There are a whole host of different ways to practise the art of car sickness but, after years of trial and error, we've found that the best method is as follows:

1) At the outset of the journey, sit in the back of the car panting like your lungs are about explode.

2) After 10 miles, start drooling and doing a lot of swallowing, but remember to keep up the panting.

3) Leave it another 20 miles before beginning to whine. You may initially find it tricky to combine whining, panting, drooling and swallowing, but keep at it and your persistence will be awarded.

4) Moments before you reach your destination, let rip with an enormous and unexpected barf. Projectile, if possible.

5) Eat the sick and then lick your owners.

Do not worry if your first attempts at high-velocity gaffing up result in dry retching and feeble barks. After all, Roman showers weren't built in a day! It took the legendary Herbie a fortnight of bingeing on Bonios to produce the vomit he is remembered for. Just be patient – and happy spewking!

Journey's start: All is well…

Out the window – a classic error

Still, a decent spread of vom

FASHION

DOGGY STYLE

Model: Lara
Fur and make-up: Jane

We love a bit of doggy-style action. And we know that you do, too. So welcome to our glossy fashion section, also known as our grovelling attempt to attract high-paying advertisers to this tawdry magazine. Note the emptiness of the pages, the vacuous attention to detail and the lack of any real ideas. Enjoy!

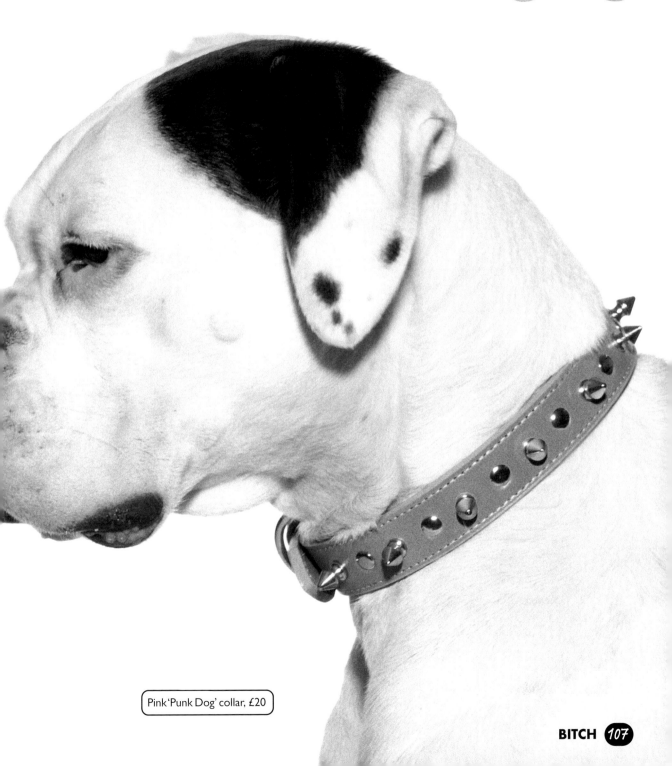

Pink 'Punk Dog' collar, £20

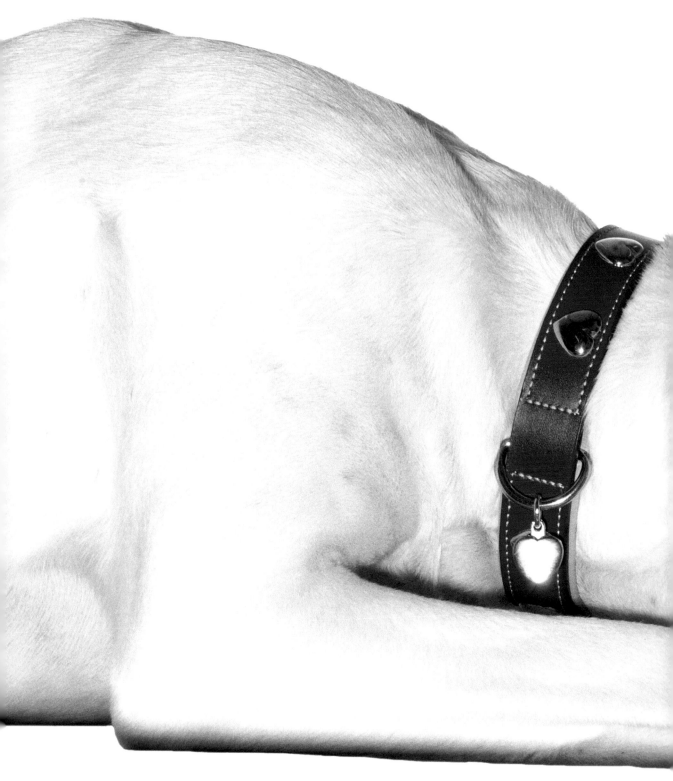

Red 'Love Is All Around' collar, £34.99

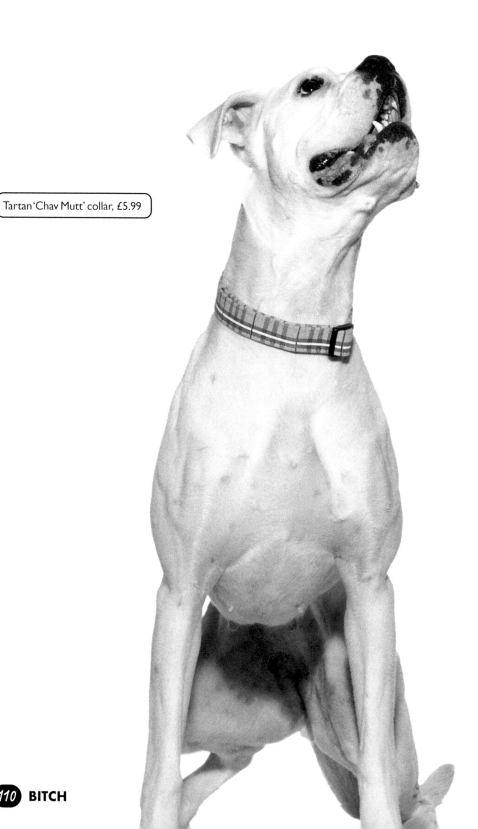

Tartan 'Chav Mutt' collar, £5.99

Blue 'Flower Power' collar, £29.99

Pink Pup Hoody, £24.99

Blue Pup Hoody, £24.99

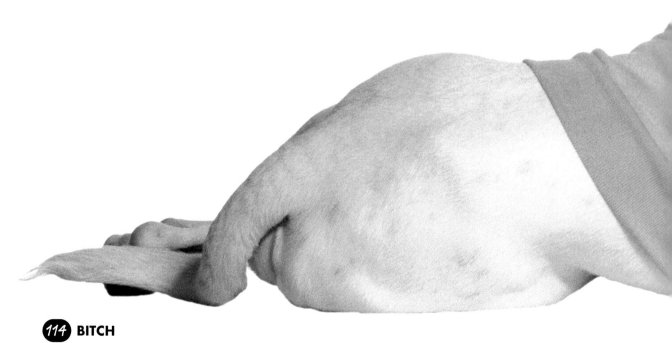

Stockists:
The Pet Shop, Main Street
The Other Pet Shop, Little Road
Also available at:
http://www.thedogweb.co.uk

CAN HE DO IT?

Health? Efficiency? You just want to gawp at naked nudies and read about sex, don't you? That's good, because in a bold move destined to go down in Big Town's small dog history books, Eric (above) has vowed to get Flossie (right) up the duff. Eric and his trainer Marshall (below) explain all

Marshall: "He's a small dog with a tiny knob, but he's got a big heart"

There was a palpable air of electricity when Eric, the pint-sized terrier from the studio flat above the hairdressing salon, announced his intention to mate with Flossie.

This is by no means an obvious match. Flossie is Big Town's famously leggy Lurcher model, who earns millions from top modelling assignments, whereas Eric is just a stupid little dog who yaps when he's tethered outside the supermarket and is rumoured to be on a special diet because he keeps throwing up.

"I know many of you will doubt my ability to pop a pup into Flossie," admitted Eric. "But I am confident of my loving skills and, now that I've managed to get Marshall on board as my trainer, the sky's the limit."

Marshall is the tough-talking lurve trainer best known for helping Perkins the Dachshund sire a huge litter of puppies with Sally the St Bernard.

"This will be easy compared to that challenge," Marshall told us yesterday. "I've got a lot of faith in this lad Eric. Sure, he's a small dog with a tiny knob, but he's got a big heart."

Shortly before going to press, we also spoke to Flossie via a video link from Glamour Town, where she is filming her first screen role in the movie *Some Dogs Running Around In The Park For An Hour And A Half*.

"I'm very excited about Eric's proposition," she said. "I know there's a huge disparity in our sizes, but we're very much in love. He's got bags of energy and I'm sure that, once he's locked on, he'll go at it like a steam engine."

Bernice the Shitzu, Eric's former lover, was not available for comment.

YES..

STICKY-UP HAIR

MANKY OLD EARS

EXTRA DROOPY JOWLS

READER TESTIMONIAL

"After running around in fields that are little more than stinking bogs of fetid mud, I find my ears get encrusted with filth and severely hamper my ability to run around in fields that are little more than stinking bogs of fetid mud. Not wanting to curtail my hobby of running around in fields that are little more than stinking bogs of fetid mud, I invested in the Fur King™ and my life has now changed for the better."
Sasha, Big Town Stinking Bogs

WE GOT PROBLEMS

Feeling troubled? There's no need to sit there whimpering, you know. Because Aunt Sally is here to help. If you're looking for sound advice, or perhaps just wanting to hear a friendly bark, write to: Aunt Sally, *Bitch* Problems Page, The Bins Round The Back Of The Butcher's Shop, Big Town, AK9 GRRR

NO SHITTER

PLEASE RELEASE ME

I'm very embarrassed about my problem, which is making me a pariah among my pals. I'm having terrible trouble loosing off my bum eggs. Sometimes I can hunch over and squeeze until my eyeballs are almost popping out of my skull and my nipsy feels as though it's going to burst, but still the train remains held up outside the station because the signals aren't working properly at King's Cross. Yesterday, I spent a full 10 minutes quivering in the dump position, stepping forwards awkwardly every few moments with my tail pointing skywards, but not one rusty nut dropped to the ground. What can I do?
Bonzo, 43 Acacia Avenue

AUNT SALLY SAYS: Bum eggs, or Oeufs de la Fond as our French cousins call them, are an essential part of the canine experience. And any dog not able to drop the kids off at the pool twice a day is facing not only a serious health issue, but social exclusion, too. Without grunty, what else are your friends going to sniff and eat when you meet up in an over-excited bundle down at the park? Try creating a more relaxing atmosphere in which to snip some loaf. Light some scented candles, put on an album by Brian Eno (we recommend Another Green World, *although success has been achieved with both* After The Heat *and* Music For Airports*) and drink a gallon of prune juice. If that doesn't get you shitting with the best of them, I don't know what will.*

SHEEP WORRYING WORRIES

I'm worried about two things. Firstly, I've heard that the government is intending to pass legislation which will, in effect, lead to sheep being interned without a proper sheep trial. I believe this is nothing but a cynical manipulation of the current climate of fear for political ends. The government is running roughshod over due process (by which I mean a farmer yelling "Come by" and blowing into an ear-piercing whistle, together with a sheepdog stalking us and making us all run into a pen of our own volition). This represents a very dangerous precedent and should not be allowed to pass. My other problem is the recent rise in the number of incidents of unprovoked sheep worrying. Why, only yesterday, I am sure that I heard shouts of "Mint sauce!" echoing across the field, followed by some giggling that sounded just like Muttley off *Wacky Races*. And while I'm on the subject, what's all this stuff I've been hearing about wolves? I find the idea of these ferocious sheep-eating dogs quite alarming, especially if they go around wearing sheep's clothing. What can I do?

Arthur Mutton, The Sheep Field

AUNT SALLY SAYS: *I'm sorry to hear about all of your worries. It must be very worrying for you. I must admit that, if I were you, I would be very worried, too. But have you heard about Bruiser's All-Night Livestock Slaughtering Club (Sheep Division)? Now that's something for you to really worry about.*

Arthur: "Worried"

BAD THING

I've done something bad.

Piper, Big Town Art School

AUNT SALLY SAYS: *Yes, you have. And you have entered it into the Turder Prize, haven't you?*

MISSING BODY MYSTERY

One day I had itchy ears and the next my entire body disappeared. I've sent you a picture to prove it. As you can see, all that is left is my head. Have you any idea what might be wrong with me?

Lulu, 368 Long Lane

AUNT SALLY SAYS: *There are two possibilities. One is you have been watching* The Invasion Of The Body Snatchers. *The other is you're suffering from LSH (Lamp Shade Head), also known as Stoppus Scratchus.*

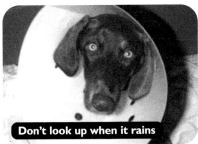
Don't look up when it rains

PAMPERED POOCH

Just because I am a Chihauhau, my movie star owner keeps putting pearl necklaces around my neck, dressing me in cashmere booties and feeding me on caviar and wild summer truffles dug from the peaty earth of the Perigord region of France. She also has my claws manicured and my choccie starfish bleached. I can't stand it. All I want to do is roll around in cow pats and get rogered senseless. What can I do?

Maria, Big Town Movie Studios

AUNT SALLY SAYS: *Grab some of that caviar and a sackful of truffles, escape through the cat flap, and meet me and Pounder outside the gasworks tonight. I'll look after the caviar and the truffles, and you can discuss the rest with Pounder canine fashion, if you get what I mean. From behind.*

Cute!

SICK PUPPY

I'm not very well.

Pups O'Puppy, 2 Little Road

AUNT SALLY SAYS: *Ahhhhh…*

PLASTERED

As you can see, I've broken my leg. I was chasing the milk float, barking like a loony and scaring milkie out of his wits, when I was hit by a car. I lay whimpering in the road until I was rescued and fixed up by the PDSA. However, my problem is that Pinko has written "Ronnie's a tosser" on my plaster cast in indelible ink. How can I get it off? Nothing seems to shift it.

Ronnie, The Tower Block, Big Town

AUNT SALLY SAYS: *I'm afraid there is no way you can remove it. And anyway, when Pinko told us he'd written that on your cast, we all laughed for 15 minutes.*

Break a leg, Ronnie

ronnie's a tosser

HORROR SCOPE

In which our strangely weird astrologer Spooky Spangles totally misunderstands the idea of a horoscope (simply because it sounds a bit like "horror scope") and, instead of making gentle and reassuring catch-all predictions, writes a load of scary stuff he's made up in his stupid little dome-shaped head. But given this is a magazine put together by dogs and its production values are therefore low (some might even describe them as slapdash), we let it pass. Indeed, we even commissioned some rather terrific "Horror Scope" graphics to accompany Spooky Spangles' deranged ramblings...

Hairies *(March 21 – April 19)*

One day, the Hairies will walk the earth. They'll come out of the sky in a spaceship thing and eat insects by the ton in a big gloopy mess of insecty legs and innards, and then they will grow stronger off the insect gloop and go on a right mad rampage of stamping on dogs. A lot of dogs will die, but canine-kind will be saved by a small group of survivors who hole up in a lighthouse and discover that sea water destroys these hirsute invaders from outer space. This will happen between the 10th and the 15th. The 16th would be a good day for starting a new business venture.

Tore Us *(April 20 – May 20)*

If you have been trying to persuade your partner to make some changes around the kennel, there's a very good chance they will suddenly turn around and their eyes will be all red, like they're glowing from the inside with some kind of evil power. They'll be frothing at the mouth and they'll leap at your neck making loud "Grrrr" noises as they try to tear your head off. It is, however, an excellent month for embarking on a new business enterprise.

Germ In Eye *(May 21 – June 20)*

This might be a good month to avoid making any decisions about travel, because you'll get some germs in your eye and they'll put ointment in your eye and then push a needle in your eye really slowly and you'll be going, like, "Agh! Agh! No! Not my eye! Agh!" and you will end up losing your eye and everything and become like a mad dog who goes around growling to yourself and biting people in the streets just like Blind "Mad Dog" Jonson who lives on the tip on that bit of old wasteland beside the sewage plant. In the meantime, that business plan you have been thinking about needs some more attention.

Canker *(June 21 – July 22)*

If you wake up to find everyone walking about wearing chemical suits and long gloves up to their elbows and breathing through tubes, this is because there's been an outbreak of a deadly virus which will make you come up in all sores and ulcers and that. It's probably going to put an end to every form of life on the planet. Try to avoid embarking on any business plans this month. It's not a good time for that sort of thing.

Leo *(July 23 – August 22)*

Leo? Oh no! Help! Help! Help! Lions on the loose! Who let the lions out? Roar! Roar! Roar! Roar! They're cats! Dirty great big, fuck-off enormous cats! They're on the loose and they're hungry for dog brain! [*Not yours, though, Spangles, you idiot. Not enough of it for them to bother with – Ed*]. A business deal that you've been waiting to hear about reaches fruition on or around the 20th.

Vertigo (August 23 – September 22)
Avoid getting tangled up in murder mysteries that have nothing to do with you this month, particularly if you have a fear of heights, because you can bet your bunny boots that something will happen that means you have to shin up a steeple or climb along a narrow and precarious ledge up a mountain. Anyway, this is a good month for turning your pin money cottage industry into something a lot more serious. Like a proper business.

Libra (September 23 – October 22)
Do not go to the Libra for the foreseeable future – even if you've got books overdue and stuff – because the two Librans that work there are evil. They're trying to take over the world and I have it on good authority that they might need a dog. On a positive note, a meeting with your bank manager will go well and you may find that the funding for your new business project will be much easier to secure than you thought.

Scorpions (October 23 – November 21)
Imagine an army of giant scorpions, each one of them 30 feet high, their massive stinging tails towering over buildings, dripping with huge doses of deadly scorpion venom. Then imagine that Godzilla comes along from the opposite direction and he's got a platoon of monster robot killing machines with him. The giant scorpions and Godzilla and his monster robot killing machines have a fight in the middle of Big Town and they smash everything up. It will be like the end of the world only probably worse. Well, that's going to happen on Thursday week, unless it's raining. Don't even think about starting that new business idea until the following Friday. Actually, you may as well leave it until the Monday. Actually, make it Tuesday, Monday's a bank holiday.

Sage It Various (November 22 – December 21)
What would happen, right, if you had all your fur shaved off, a load of sage and onion stuffing squished up your arse, an apple put in your gob, and then you were put in the oven at gas mark eight for five hours? I'll tell you what would happen. Roast dog, that's what, and that's what everybody will be eating this month. You mark my words. An opportunity to launch a new business venture will come your way soon afterwards, though.

Capri Corn On The Cob (December 22 – January 19)
The Jolly Green Giant will ram-raid the convenience store on the Big Town High Street this month in his 1975 Ford Capri and he'll steal all the tins of dog food and replace them with corn on the cobs and he'll be going "Ho! Ho! Ho!" Terrible scenes. This might be a good time to attend to any business matters that have been troubling you lately.

A Queer Hairies (January 20 – February 18)
This would be something like the Hairies (see above) only much weirder. They'll conjure up packs of zombie dogs from the insect gloop that the Hairies have left lying around the place and these dead-but-not-dead mutts will roam around the recreation ground. Except on Sundays. Which means Sunday is the best day to start thinking about quitting your job and going it alone, pursuing your own vision and being your own boss in a new business.

Fish (February 19 – March 20)
This one's when you go for a swim and you realise that the crazy scientist with the long beard has let out loads of mutant piranha and they've been multiplying by the million. When they sniff you doing the doggy paddle, they'll come and strip your skellington of every shred of flesh, even your bumhole. You won't stand a chance. Luckily for you, business matters take a turn for the better when a letter out of the blue offers you a start-up loan for that business you've been thinking about in recent weeks.

Spooky Spangles: Impaired visionary

READERS' MATES

If you really love them, send us a picture of them. Then we can all enjoy the contours of their feet and marvel at the way their two legs hold them up like that. We can also all imagine the various delicious odours of their sweaty plates. We pay a bone for every photo we print

Herman, 712 Long Lane
"My owner runs 10 miles every day. Oh, the stink! You'd love it, I tell you."

Bilbo, Big Town Farm
"My mistress wears these beautiful green wellies day in, day out. They're fantastic. They're always teeming with all manner of pongs. Rotting vegetation is a constant top stink, although occasionally there's also the ming of manure."

Polly, 31 The Villas
"I love my master to bits. He's got big black shoes and they sometimes smell of cheese that's gone off, exactly like that Edam he left in the fridge for six months so that it went like rock."

Jack, the Chip Shop
"My master paints his toenails and wears stilettos. He is called Davina, but only at weekends. His feet smell of chip fat and too much talcum powder."

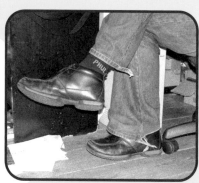

Lulu, 35 Acacia Avenue
"My owner Paulie only changes his socks once a week. Once a month during the winter. The whiff is enough to make you heave. Lovely!"

Ozzy, 18 Little Road
"These are Pixie's feet. She's five. I like them because they smell of flowers. And cheese. Cheesy flowers! Mmmm."

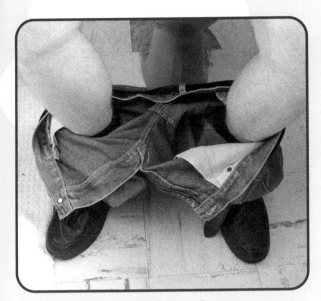

Bob, Big Town Public Conveniences
"I can't even begin to describe the cornucopia of pongs I was enjoying when I took this photo. I'll leave it to your imagination. As long you imagine cheesy grunty."

Pongo, 22a Big Town High Street
"Here's me with my mate. There are no stinky feet around here, just some prime bitch ass."

ALSO FROM THE CREATORS OF

BITCH...

E WHEEL
THE JOURNAL FOR RODENTS & SMALL FURRIES WORLDWIDE · Issue 2

A CLEANER CAGE

POLYGAMY FOR BEGINNERS

SPECIAL REDUCED PRICE

EMPIRES: ARE THEY <u>REALLY</u> WORTH IT?

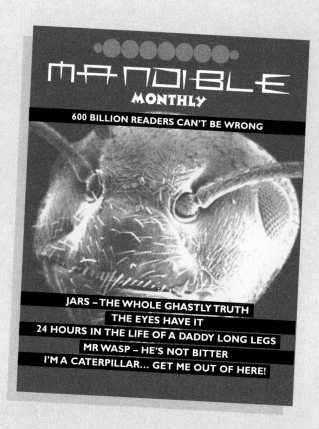

MANDIBLE MONTHLY

600 BILLION READERS CAN'T BE WRONG

JARS – THE WHOLE GHASTLY TRUTH
THE EYES HAVE IT
24 HOURS IN THE LIFE OF A DADDY LONG LEGS
MR WASP – HE'S NOT BITTER
I'M A CATERPILLAR... GET ME OUT OF HERE!

BITCH CLASSIFIEDS

BARKTONES.COM

Call **WOOF** for:
I'm sure I saw a cat

Call **WOOOF** for:
I think that's the postie

Call **WOOOOFF** for:
Some bastard's blowing
on a whistle

Call **WOOOOFFF** for:
Some bastard's chained
me up outside

Call **WOOOOOFFFF** for:
I'm sure I heard something
six miles away

Call **WOOOOOOFFFFF** for:
I'm just gonna bark for
no good reason

INDECISIVE?
UNCERTAIN?
CAN'T MAKE UP YOUR MIND?
DON'T KNOW WHICH WAY TO TURN?
Me neither!

HELP!!

IF LOST RETURN TO: 1332-664-4001

Come Poo Dancing

Learn how to lay neat lines of
turds in a friendly atmosphere

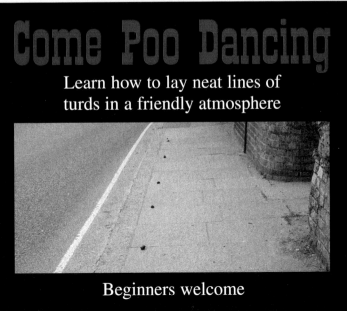

Beginners welcome

Bitch was conceived and created by Steven Appleton, Christopher Dawes, Mark Roland and Paul Thompson
Studio photography by Dave Guttridge at The Photographic Unit, Norwich
Elzie Crysler by Steven Weissman

Support and assistance: Emily Groom, Kaoru Sakurai, Susie Mair, Jan Newell and Antony Topping

Dog people: Amy Barratt, Philippa Biddle, Daniel & Evie Brandish, Sheila Buckingham, Billy Butcher, Bob & Carolyn Carter, Rebecca Clinton, Jane & Matthew Colman, Angie Cook, Dina Doerfel, Stephen Franklin, Nigel Hannant, Simon Harris, Pat & Steve Harris, Anthony Harrison, Judi Hayes, Jo & Si Lloyd, Jean Matthews, Kerry Negus at Bounce Records, Notty Nottingham, Claire Owen, Andy Pearmain, Frances Plume, Janice Pratt, Bill Read, Grace Richardson, Jane Shakesby, J Sharp, John Skinner, Jill Smith, Dick & Lillian Thompson, Marie Twentyman, Pip & Lucy Whittle, Frances Willis, Ginny Wolper, Carl Wright, Rueben Youngblood, and Damyon & Sarah.

THAT'S YER LOT

TRANSWORLD PUBLISHERS
61-63 Uxbridge Road, London W5 5SA, a division of The Random House Group Ltd

RANDOM HOUSE AUSTRALIA (PTY) LTD
20 Alfred Street, Milsons Point, Sydney, New South Wales 2061, Australia

RANDOM HOUSE NEW ZEALAND LTD
18 Poland Road, Glenfield, Auckland 10, New Zealand

RANDOM HOUSE SOUTH AFRICA (PTY) LTD
Endulini, 5a Jubilee Road, Parktown 2193, South Africa

Published 2005 by Bantam Press, a division of Transworld Publishers

A catalogue record for this book is available from the British Library.
ISBN 0593 054997

Printed in Germany

Papers used by Transworld Publishers are natural, recyclable products made from wood grown in sustainable forests. The manufacturing processes conform to the environmental regulations of the country of origin.